# FLORIDA PHOTOGENESIS

THE • WORK • OF • CREATIVE • AND • EXPERIMENTAL • PHOTOGRAPHERS • IN • FLORIDA

Text by
**Robert W. Fichter**

Interview with
**Van Deren Coke**

Florida State University Museum of Fine Arts
October 6-November 19, 2000

Appleton Museum of Art, Ocala, Florida
February 23-April 22, 2001

Southeast Museum of Photography, Daytona Beach, Florida
October 2001-January 2002

---

**Florida State University Museum of Fine Arts**
**School of Visual Arts & Dance**

*Florida Photogenesis: The Work of Creative and Experimental Photographers in Florida* was organized by the Florida State University Museum of Fine Arts with grant assistance from the National Endowment for the Arts and the Florida Arts Council. Educational Programming is supported by The Junior Woman's Club of Tallahassee and through the Communiversity Partnership—Tallahassee Cultural Services, Cultural Resources Commission.

Cover: Todd Walker, *The Swamp*, digital file, c. 1990s. Courtesy of the Todd Walker Estate.

## MUSEUM OF FINE ARTS STAFF

Allys Palladino-Craig, Director
Viki D. Thompson Wylder, Curator of Education
Jean D. Young, Registrar / Fiscal Officer
Becky Jones, Coordinator, Appleton Projects
Mark Fletcher, Preparator / Photographer
Michael Sperow, Preparator / Graphics
Assistants:
Harry Bleattler, Julie Bohannon, Gina Kim,
Barb Solomon, Lisa Thorik, Marian Wooten

## VOLUNTEERS AND INTERNS

James Sweeney, Coordinator • Miguel Amador • Laura Askins • Dongyol Baik • Kim Brazerol • Sara Chumbley • Leslie Cohen • Alden Drewry • Katherine Forbes • Audrey Gay • Colleen Gorny • Morgan Hanner • Veronica Harris • Colleen Jazrawi • Lori Johnson • Linda Kaye Johnson • Cindy Killingsworth • Leslie Letchworth • Susan Mann • Vicki Mariner • Cara Norman • Mary Pierce • Melissa Ray • Michela Restina • Barbara Schauwecker • Christine Steffens • Rebecca Wagner • Pam Wallheiser • Adam Woods • J. Thomas Wylder

## MUSEUM PRESS

Editor-in-Chief: A. Palladino-Craig
Graphic Design: Julienne T. Mason
Printer: Progressive Printing, Jacksonville


ISBN 1-889282-09-X

## CONTENTS



## PROJECT SUPPORT AND ORGANIZATION

*Florida Photogenesis* was organized by the Florida State University Museum of Fine Arts with grant assistance from the National Endowment for the Arts and the Florida Arts Council. Educational Programming is supported by The Junior Woman's Club of Tallahassee and through the Communiversity Partnership—Tallahassee Cultural Services, Cultural Resources Commission. Concept: Robert W. Fichter, Professor of Art. Project Curatorial Support: A. Palladino-Craig, Becky L. Jones. Project Grantwriter and Editor—Allys Palladino-Craig; Appleton Coordinator—Becky L. Jones; Museum Press Design—Julienne T. Mason; Fiscal Officer—Jean Young; Educational Programming—Viki D. Thompson Wylder; Chief Preparator—Mark Fletcher; Senior Assistant Preparator—Michael Sperow. Publication Photography: Jon Nalon (*Bailey* 31, *Van Deren Coke* 8, 34, 35, 55) and Artists, unless otherwise noted.

This program is sponsored in part by the State of Florida, Department of State,
Katherine Harris, Secretary of State,
Division of Cultural Affairs—
**Florida Arts Council**

The Museum gratefully acknowledges the support of the
**National Endowment for the Arts**

Educational Programming for K-12 and Seniors
underwritten in part by grants from the
**Communiversity Partnership**
**Tallahassee Cultural Services**
and
**The Tallahassee Junior Woman's Club**

Funding: Museum Press publication was supported by funding generated from private contributions and public grant funds. Other Museum funding derives from the School of Visual Arts & Dance, J. L. Draper, Dean; fund-raising by the Museum on behalf of its programming includes the support of the Membership.

## LENDERS TO THE EXHIBITION

Canyon Cinema

Linda and Moses Rodin

Marsha Orr Contemporary Art

Signature Gallery

Southeast Museum of Photography

Tricia Collins Contemporary Art

Melanie Walker, Estate of Todd Walker

The Artists' Studios

## BENEFACTORS

The National Endowment for the Arts

The Florida Arts Council

Communiversity Partnership—Tallahassee Cultural Services

The Tallahassee Junior Woman's Club

## ARTISTS

Oscar Bailey

George Blakely

Van Deren Coke

Robert W. Fichter

Virgil Mirano

Doug Prince

Evon Streetman

Tyler Turkle

Jerry Uelsmann

Todd Walker

Wallace Wilson

David Yager

# FLORIDA AND THE ACADEMIC MEDICI

Over the years, we have come to rely on the faith and support of the Florida Arts Council and once more, we are most pleased to note that we have been rewarded on this project as well. It is also extremely gratifying to know that our programs have a validity not only in Florida, but beyond state boundaries. It gives me great pleasure to thank the peer review process at the National Endowment for the Arts, specifically the Heritage and Preservation panel, for investing so generously in *Florida Photogenesis*, the concept created by Professor Robert Fichter, Florida State University Department of Art. I am also proud to announce that this book will be distributed nationally by the University of Washington Press, reaching not only the interested public but countless artists and art historians through libraries both public and private.

Robert Fichter has cast a long shadow in terms of active service in cultural initiatives across the state. His studio work has been the entrée for him to numerous grants and awards, and in terms of influence for generations of students, he is one of the acknowledged pioneers in the realm of experimental photography—to which Van Deren Coke insisted, and rightly so, that the adjective "creative" be linked. As Fichter will tell you, he is not alone, though it is through his understanding of Florida photographic history that this exhibition has been mounted. Serving as contact and mentor, he has made it possible for this museum to gather works from not only himself, but eleven other artists whose careers have meant so much to the field in Florida academic institutions and in the much larger art world. We have had the interesting experience of being able to bracket the careers of these artists with works created in their early days of working in Florida right up to their current careers. They are a peripatetic lot—several traveled to new posts, others traveled and taught as visiting artists while maintaining their Florida positions. In the time-honored tradition of artist-scholars, they have shared their insights and their technical achievements with students who will no doubt cross and re-cross the United States, if not the world, ever enlarging the sphere of influence in our electronic age where few pockets of civilization are left untouched. Yet, ultimately, one point that Professor Fichter draws is that the great freedom to research and expand intellectual horizons was due to the support system of the academic institutions and to the spirit of enterprise and enquiry fostered there—the universities in essence underwriting so much of American creativity in this era, just as the Medici once did in the European past.

With much pride, and mindful of the vital advocacy of our grant-agency supporters, we open the doors of this exhibition in the first of its venues, Florida State University, Robert Fichter's home ground. On behalf of our Dean, Jerry L. Draper, both museums of the School of Visual Arts and Dance—the Museum of Fine Arts on the main campus and the Appleton Museum of Art in Ocala—now welcome you to *Florida Photogenesis*.

Allys Palladino-Craig
Director, Museum of Fine Arts

## AUTHOR'S ACKNOWLEDGMENTS

I would like to thank my wife, Nancy Smith Fichter, both for her encouragement and for her skillful editing of my text. In addition, I thank the Museum staff for their commitment and the high level of organization that they have brought to the project. This completes a quartet of exhibitions in which I have explored ideas about the manipulation of the photographic image by artists. Without the ongoing support of Dean Jerry Draper, none of those exhibitions would have occurred. Finally, I would like to thank Roald Nasgaard, Chair, and the Art Department faculty for their continued support of the photography program over the years.

—Robert W. Fichter

## FLORIDA PHOTOGENESIS: THE WORK OF CREATIVE AND EXPERIMENTAL PHOTOGRAPHERS IN FLORIDA

*Robert W. Fichter*

*If Todd Walker were alive today he would say that this exhibition is about "funny picture makers."*

The title of the exhibition, *Florida Photogenesis: The Work of Creative and Experimental Photographers in Florida*, may indeed be too broad, for as with its underground rivers there are many different streams of photography that have arisen in Florida. There have certainly been many fine artists / teachers supported by the state university system who have used photography as their creative means. There were of course those who used the medium in the straight tradition; however if we look at the work of artists in the academic institutions, we can see that there was a particular group of artists / photographers, beginning with Van Deren Coke's presence at the University of Florida in 1958, and extending to Florida State University and the University of South Florida, who were committed to very different agendas than those held by more traditional photographic artists. Although urban avant-garde art centers such as Chicago and Los Angeles offered support for such experimental activities, in the southeast only the academic institutions in Florida were actively supporting artists who were stretching the boundaries of photography.

In this text I want to lay out lines of thought about creative and experimental photography as manifested by the artists included in this show. Additionally the obvious photogenetic swapping that has occurred among the group should be evident.

### VAN DEREN COKE

*The University of Florida, 1958-1961*

In the late 1950s, when Van Deren Coke came to Florida the classic American modernist[1] model of what a photograph should look like was highly developed, i.e., black and white, continuous tone, great depth of field, objects in focus from the front to the back of the picture plane. The work was usually done with an 8x10" view camera to yield an image of the highest resolution possible with the use of a normal lens.[2] All this was in reaction to the pictorialist movement in photography,

---

1 High modernist theory presented the field of photography as a territory defined by the single frame and unmanipulated photographic image. The photograph was seen as truth, a single moment in time, frozen and plucked out of the flux of change. It was an activity separate from all other art forms, sometimes yielding a poetic image, but usually representing exact reality. When a poetic image was produced by this aesthetic system, it was framed in terms of a personal, subjective revelatory act. In the mid-1960s, a time of less corporate ownership of our cultural lives, this seemed a somewhat hospitable position. By the 1990s, modernism had been dethroned and was being routinely attacked by critics such as Abigail Solomon-Godeau, Hilton Kramer, and Allan Sekula, who were confronted with the large mass of photographs being produced by university trained artists. Excerpts from *Photography at the Dock*, Abigail Solomon-Godeau (1991), pages 82 and 87: "Art photography...privileged subjectivity and the use of formal properties to express that subjectivity." [82] "Implicit in the notion of the photographer's expressive mediation of the world through the use of his or her instrument is a related constellation of assumptions: the subjectivity of vision and the camera as medium of that subjectivity; the sovereignty of authorship; the belief that the meaning of a photograph exists autonomously within the boundaries of its frame. That those assumptions are coeval with modernism—what Walter Benjamin called the theology of art—and are, in fact, its photographic analog, have to a considerable extent determined the ethos as well as the fortunes of art photography." [87]

2 A normal lens approximates the angle of view of the human eye, having neither wide angle nor telephoto distortion in its perspective view.

which had favored tone and form over high resolution. Pictorialism, highly popular in America up until the late 1930s, was in fact an obvious attempt to emulate many of the qualities of late nineteenth century painting and thus was anathema to modernist critics who wanted to free photography from the past.

As a teenager, Coke had driven to the West Coast to meet Edward Weston, who was at that time the acknowledged leader of the modernist school of photography. Weston took a liking to him and invited him to stay for several weeks. Coke also met Ansel Adams and others and began collecting their work. Having grown up in Lexington, Kentucky, the son of a successful hardware store owner, he involved himself in the Lexington Camera Club, a group of people seriously interested in photography as a fine art. He was a friend and teacher of Ralph Eugene Meatyard, whose work, a sort of Southern Gothic vein of imagery, was akin to the work of New Orleans photographer Clarence John Laughlin. This work is now largely forgotten, but it influenced a number of younger photographers such as Wallace Wilson, Jerry Uelsmann and myself, when it appeared in *Aperture*, the only serious publication about American photography at that time. Coke, though deeply schooled in the modernist tradition, supported the opening up of the language of photography to encompass many other variations. Although Edward Weston and Ansel Adams were his early teachers and mentors, his interactions with Man Ray in Paris in 1960 encouraged him to experiment with a greater freedom in his printmaking. He searched for a method of escaping the excessive reality of the photograph. Tom Barrow, in an introduction to a 1981 exhibition of Coke's early work, quotes the artist's statement on the development of his working methods: "Through experimentation, I found that flashing on a white light in a darkroom while the print is still in the developer gave me an image that was allusive and mysterious but not completely divorced from a feeling of reality—a feeling that was a very necessary ingredient for me."

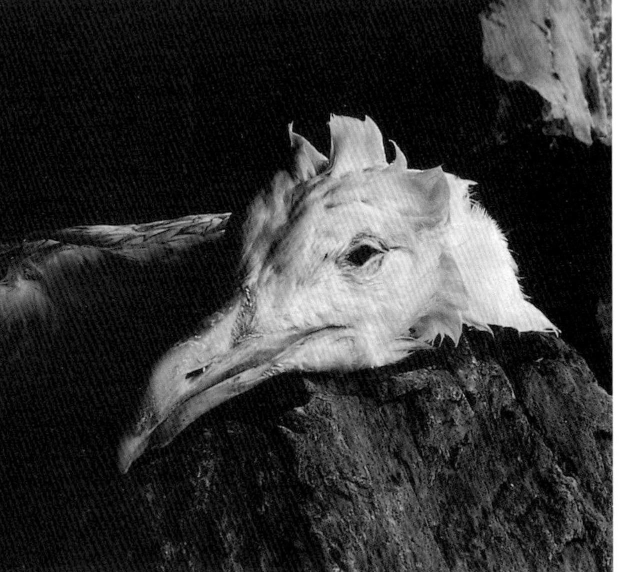
Van Deren Coke, *Dying Sea Gull*, 1958, silver gelatin print, 10⅓x11¾ inches.

Coke had been hired to teach in the Department of Art at the University of Florida by Clinton Adams, one of America's pioneer lithographers, who had a printmaker's sympathy for photography. Printmakers at that time were only slightly higher on the art community's social scale than were photographers. Before arriving in Florida, Coke had been mentored at Indiana University by Henry Hope, an urbane art historian, who dealt with international art issues for UNESCO. Although still working very much in the modernist vein, Van Deren Coke showed evidence of change in his personal work; he might speak of surrealism but in muted tones. Later in the 1960s, these changes became much more blatant, with the use of a flash of light on his prints during development and the use of 19th-century found negatives along with his own, etc.

Coke's major publication, *The Painter and the Photograph* (1964), examined the relationships that painters had had with photographic source material. It appeared at a time in which there was great denial in the painting community about the use of photographs. Coke's book documented through side-by-side illustrations how painters had used photography since its invention.

At the University of Florida, Coke taught photography and art history. Shortly after Coke's arrival, Clinton Adams left to direct the Tamarind Institute in Los Angeles and then was hired to be the Dean of the School of Fine Arts at the University of New Mexico. He called Coke to come to New Mexico where he headed the Department of Art as well as the Museum. Before he left Florida, Coke hired Jerry Uelsmann to teach photography and design at the University because he liked what he saw in Uelsmann's portfolio: great technical skills and a budding sense of surreal poetic vision based on subtle manipulations (such as multiple printing by means of *blends* and *negative sandwiches*) that went beyond the borders of the modernist straight photograph.

## JERRY UELSMANN
*The University of Florida, 1960-1997*

Jerry Uelsmann espoused a postvisualization concept which was in reaction to Ansel Adams' previsualization theory. Adams held that if one learned one's craft in a highly methodical fashion and developed one's negatives correctly, then it was possible to previsualize what the final print would look like in terms of tones. That attitude continued and reinforced the dominant photo ideology that the camera worker is locked in a direct relationship to any given moment in time. Uelsmann's concept of postvisualization was that photographers could be released to create their own time and space. Coke had brought high modernist photography to Florida; Uelsmann brought surrealism, a struggling form of modernism, and his students brought postmodernism to the scene. Uelsmann encouraged his students to experiment with image making in the broadest ways: in focus, out of focus, multiple exposures, time exposures, new surfaces, etc. As a student studying with Uelsmann, I was once asked by another student, "Don't you think photography is too limited by its means?" That seemed a strange question to me. The concept of photography laid out by Uelsmann was that of an experimental art form that transcended the single frame boundary and was in fact just another mark making means for the artist. This concept was influenced by the teaching of Henry Holmes Smith, a leading theoretician of progressive thought in creative photography. Uelsmann had met Smith at Indiana University, after studying at the Rochester Institute of Technology with Minor White and Ralph Hattersly; he was not a naive "photo-techie" when he ended up in one of Smith's graduate classes. It may be helpful at this point to take note of Smith's own history. In Chicago, Smith had worked for Lazlo Moholy-Nagy, who was directing the Chicago Institute of Design (the "New Bauhaus"); he had found Moholy-Nagy's modern radical attitudes toward photography much to his liking. Smith was soon setting up a darkroom and teaching color photography for him at the Institute; therefore Smith brought a Bauhausian attitude to his teaching at Indiana University and fused it with an American sensibility for the poetics of imagery. Influenced by the writings of I.A. Richards, Smith taught his students how to look at photography by "learning to read a photograph." Henry Holmes Smith's Zen master question, "What should a photo look like?" opened Jerry Uelsmann to the active poetic mind.

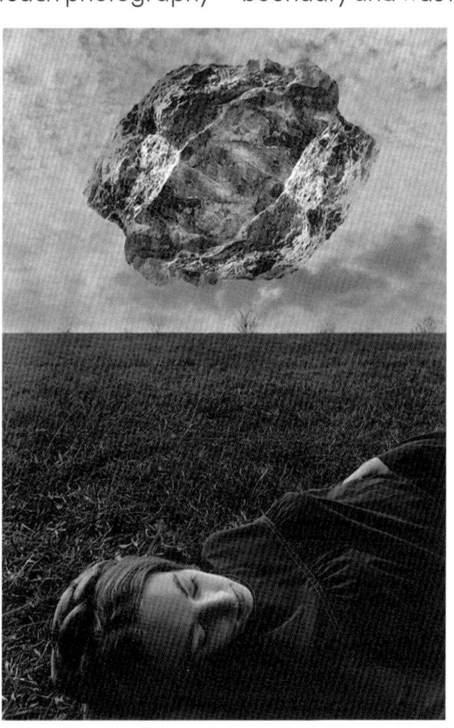

Jerry Uelsmann, *Magritte's Touchstone*, 1965, silver gelatin print, 16x20 inches.

Once during a conversation with Smith,

Uelsmann ridiculed a multiple print done by a well-known Chicago experimental photographer, and Smith challenged him to try the method himself before he so easily dismissed it. In the darkroom Uelsmann found that his brilliant, comedic associative thought processes could blend images in ways that allowed him to make symbols about the human condition. Such constructs yielded signs with which to make metaphors. Beaumont Newhall, the director of the George Eastman House Museum and a leading photographic historian, was at first appalled by Uelsmann's blends and perceived him as a resurrection of Oscar G. Rejlander and Henry Peach Robinson, two nineteenth century "art photographers" who used similar techniques and who had been consigned to the dust bin of history by Newhall. The years following Uelsmann's first publications, however, were those of the blooming of the postmodernist photo aesthetic; and Newhall soon came to see Uelsmann's blended images, which retained deep Renaissance perspective while breaking the time frame of the high modernist canon, as *real photographs*. Uelsmann in fact today seems closely related to the Surrealists and to the Pre-Raphaelite painters in his constructed metaphoric search for meaning.

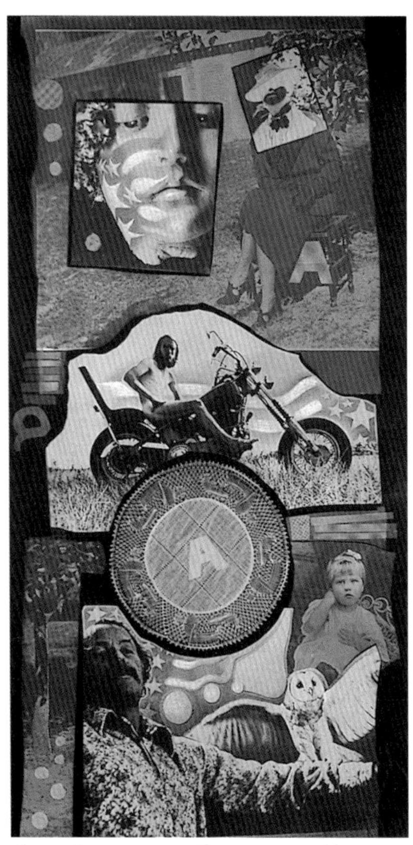

Evon Streetman, *All American blueprint*, 1978, blueprint, hand coloring, 20x34 inches.

When Uelsmann left Indiana to teach at the University of Florida, the big boom of interest in photography was occurring all across the country. During his first year at Florida, he was assigned to teach a design class as well as an introduction to photography. His great comic charm and the presentation of a simple photographic method (2¼" format cameras, using slow black and white film to achieve fine quality 8x10" prints with available light) allowed his students to accomplish excellent results without the traditional struggle to master a 4x5" view camera with all its trappings (dark cloth, tripod, film holders, studio lighting). His teaching was also characterized by insights into the history and criticism of photography; he encouraged a sense of inquiry that drew from the best of Henry Holmes Smith's concepts about creative photography and that was augmented by his own provocative, amusing and irreverent thoughts. Quickly his classes filled to overflowing so that he was soon teaching only photography. Although he based his studio in Florida, he aggressively courted the New York photo media establishment; his Christmas cards went out to everyone of any importance in the photo world and quickly became collectors' items, since his vision seemed to strike many chords. Uelsmann used abandoned nineteenth century photographic art practices such as multiple negatives in creating single prints in the manner of Rejlander and Robinson, and he did such a skillful job of creating his visual fables using Renaissance perspective principles that his images moved directly into the American psyche. Although Uelsmann's aesthetic intention was unique and quite different from that of Ansel Adams, his work shares, oddly enough, some of Adams' characteristic strengths, i.e., beautiful clarity of focus, unbelievable depth of field and detailed backgrounds. Uelsmann broke the time honored photographic relationship between time and space. Although he does not directly use any digital technology in his work, he is seen by many to be the Leonardo da Vinci of Photoshop.

## EVON STREETMAN

*Florida State University, 1964-1971; The University of Florida, 1978-1999*

Evon Streetman, who received her art training at Florida State University, returned from a stint in New York working as a professional photographer to open a portrait studio in Tallahassee. Her technical control of the medium and her ability to make portraits of striking intensity soon made her a recognized leader in the field. She was asked by the Chair of the Art Department at Florida State University to create a photography course. She began attending national photographic conferences about creative photography and soon realized that she had a whole set of artistic talents that could be applied to the making of photographs that transcended the traditional. She began to use a variety of non-silver processes; then she moved on to painting with air brush on color prints, increasing the scale of the images as she went along. In addition to setting up a photography program at Florida State University, Streetman started a photography program at the Penland School of Crafts in Penland, North Carolina, to be held during the summers. In 1971 she was invited to move to Penland on a full-time basis. She went to North Carolina and remained there until she got a phone call in 1978 from Jerry Uelsmann asking her to teach at the University of Florida.

Streetman offers the following artist's statement which clearly articulates her ideas and work methods:

"Most of my work uses the landscape as a subternatural basis and usually posits two or three layers of intentions.

"This begins with a blatant interest in the beauty of natural things and then moves to the second layer which deals with an emotional response born from my most precious memories of a rural childhood. This fecund ecology of the thirties, now more and more, only exists in my memory.

"The third layer is the intellectual analysis of that space, the picture as an object and the formal treatment of the picture plane with the blending of totally photographic information and totally imagined information. This pastiche of real and invented subject is a subterfuge that hopefully will please and confuse the viewer in a way that highlights questions about our conceits of observation in every respect.

"In the intervening time between pictures and fishing, this all provides a visual RUBIK'S CUBE for my brain while I watch the referent slowly disappear."

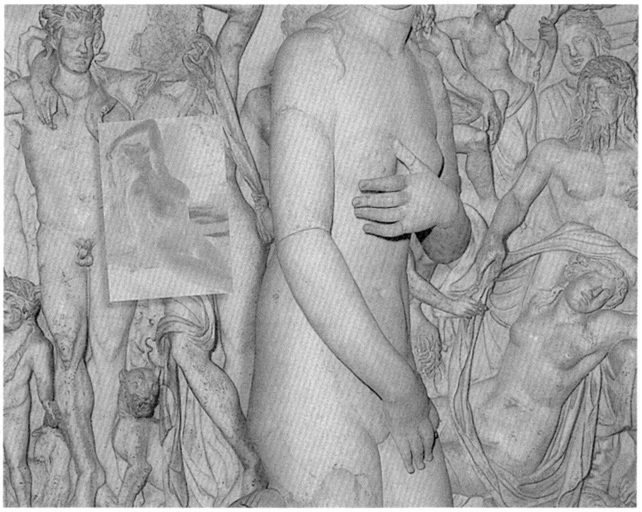

Doug Prince, *Body Image #8*, 1999, inkjet print, 11x14 inches.

Streetman is a great Southern storyteller in both her pictures and in her classroom. She offers us a rich legacy. During her long career she has worked through a variety of methods and techniques. In every instance her strong sense of being emerges and engages us in a wonderful way.

## DOUGLAS PRINCE

*The University of Florida, 1968-1976*

Douglas Prince joined the faculty of the University of Florida in 1968, a time when both the student population and the demand for photography had increased. Prince's early training had been based in the tradition of straight photography, but he had soon felt the restraints of the single straight image and for one of his undergraduate exhibitions hung "pieces of weathered wood, rusty metal and wire, old gloves and dead birds" instead of photographs of such objects. In 1965, he was introduced to orthographic film, which is used in the printing industry to record high contrast information but which can also be processed to yield a continuous tone positive image, a transparent photograph. He began making photo sculptures and in his graduation exhibition he "put together a show which consisted of photo-sculptures with layers of film (some with mirrored surfaces), film overlays, several different types of stereo constructions, images with parts animated by electric motors and prints of multiple-negative blends." Arriving at the University of Florida to teach the undergraduate beginning classes, Prince found an open environment in which he could continue to explore the widening form of photography. He refined his early experiments by taking photography into three dimensions. He consolidated his means and materials, producing exquisite 5x5" boxes of Plexiglas and film transparencies. His flat prints, *blended* images, might be seen in the umbra of Uelsmann's prints, but the boxes allowed him to step into an arena of his own. They draw upon the same psychological sources as his blended imagery but play more directly with the real world. The fact that he was exposed to the work of Jack Nichelson, a fellow faculty member, may well have had a beneficial effect. Nichelson, who had also studied with Henry Smith at Indiana University at the same time as did Uelsmann and who had joined the faculty at the University of Florida to teach design at the same time Uelsmann had arrived to teach photography, chose to set aside his interest in photography and follow his interest in Joseph Cornell's three dimensional worlds. He has subsequently created a distinctive body of work, flawlessly crafted, utilizing found objects and imagery in a box format. This could only have increased Prince's confidence in creating his own small worlds.

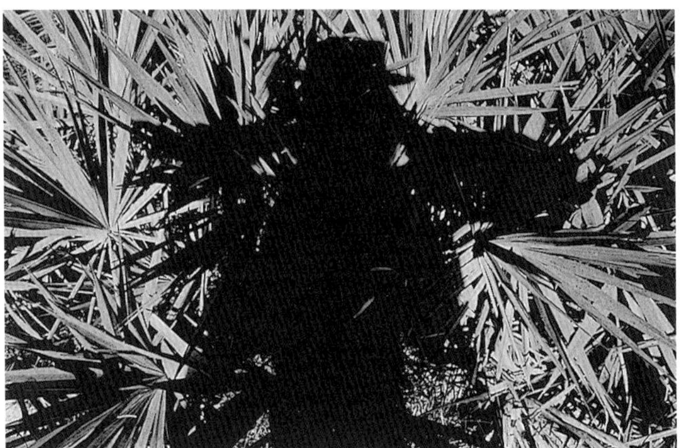

Oscar Bailey, *Me—Shadow Series*, 1974, silver gelatin print, 5¾x8½ inches.

## OSCAR BAILEY

*The University of South Florida, 1969-1985*

Oscar Bailey established the photography program at the University of South Florida in 1969. When hired by Donald Saff to teach photography at the University of South Florida, Bailey was already a well-known photographer. In his early days he had been an admirer of the work of Edward Weston and Minor White. In 1962 he attended one of Henry Holmes Smith's teaching conferences at Indiana University; out of this meeting the Society for Photographic Education was created the next year in Rochester, New York, and became the networking institution for American art photographers. Bailey started using a wide-format banquet camera in 1967 (his Cirkut photographs); this was an antique camera with a spring-driven gear system that moved the lens and the film of the camera, producing images up to 60 inches in length. The panoramic (180 degree view) image, originally developed to make landscape views and valued for recording formal gatherings of large groups of people, was not being used by artists. Bailey's use of this format heralded the current craze for such a format which finds its expression in both inexpensive throw-away panoramic cameras and the "stitched" 360 degree panoramas being produced via computer techniques. Bailey also worked with photo emulsion to create constructions that thrust his images back into the real world.

## TODD WALKER

*The University of Florida, 1970-1977*

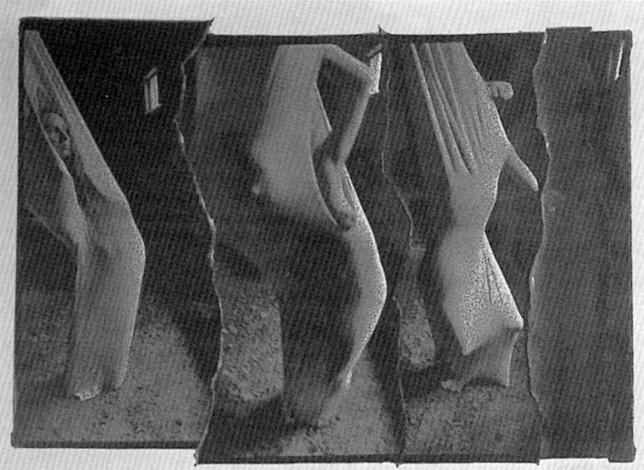

Todd Walker, *Francine, dancing*, 1972, silkscreen, 14½ x 19 inches.

After Douglas Prince left the University of Florida, Todd Walker was asked to join the faculty. Walker, who was a legendary professional photographer in Los Angeles, had been moving toward his own personal vision quest after a successful career shooting photographs for Chevrolet ads and other commercial ventures. He had begun experimenting with a variety of alternative photographic processes (gum printing, blue printing, colotype, offset printing, silk screen); and he started a systematic investigation of image manipulation through the solarization of images to distort and render alternative realities. (He was the Giotto of Photoshop.) Walker had the ability to read any text about photographic processes and then be able to duplicate the process or reinvent it. When asked how he did that, he would simply say with a sly grin, "Well...it's just like everything else..." In the '60s and '70s Walker took the nude female form as his text and always read into those forms a vibrant expression of color and energy. In the 1980s and 1990s, he photographed rocks and plant forms; and, using elementary early computer machine code, he taught himself how to turn any pixel on his screen into any color he wanted it to be. He used code taken from encryption programs and from 3-D land mapping programs and ran his images through those codes to see what they would look like. Once I heard him say, "I can do in 15 minutes with the computer what used to take me three weeks to do with film." He had no use for any user friendly interfaces such as those developed by Apple and Microsoft. He could launch one of his hand coded pieces of software and take an image apart long before Photoshop could even look at that same image. It's no wonder Adobe never offered him any support. He laughed at the slowness of their efforts.

## ROBERT W. FICHTER

*Florida State University, 1972-present*

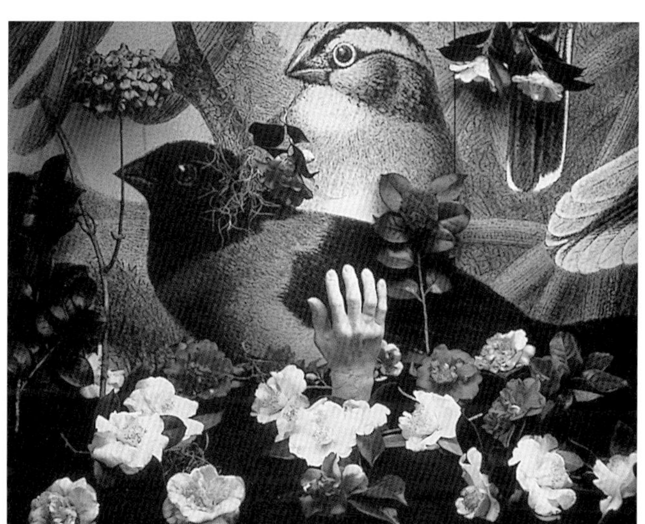

Robert W. Fichter, *Hand of Man*, 1984, cibachrome, 35x28½ inches.

As I look back on my professional life, I clearly see a trace line from Moholy-Nagy through Henry Holmes Smith, through Jerry Uelsmann to myself. (The rhetoric of experimentalism was our chosen tongue.) When I studied with Uelsmann at the University of Florida in the early 1960s, the colors of photography were black and white, and continuous tone 8x10" prints were the standard of the day. At that time a degree in art from the University of Florida had to be in painting, sculpture, printmaking or design, *not* photography. On the contemporary national scene, photography was not collected by most major museums and certainly no major artist worked in photography, at least as far as art critics and the mass media were concerned. Today, of course, photography is considered to be one of the "hottest" media in which an artist can work. Studying with Uelsmann helped me to feel the freedom to photograph anything that seemed relevant to the way I felt, a freedom I've never lost. Uelsmann recognized my radical attitude toward photography and he still says, "Fichter steps on his negatives before he prints them." After I completed a BFA degree in painting and printmaking, Uelsmann sent me to study with his former mentor, Henry Holmes Smith, at Indiana University, where I became involved in using various historical and alternative processes. I completed my MFA degree there and then accepted a position as junior curator at the Eastman House Museum of Photography under the direction of Nathan Lyons. That institution was then launching a series of exhibitions that were to define photography in a much broader form than it had previously been viewed in America. The experience exposed me to a huge archive of images; it was like being let loose as one of the 'raiders of the lost Ark.'

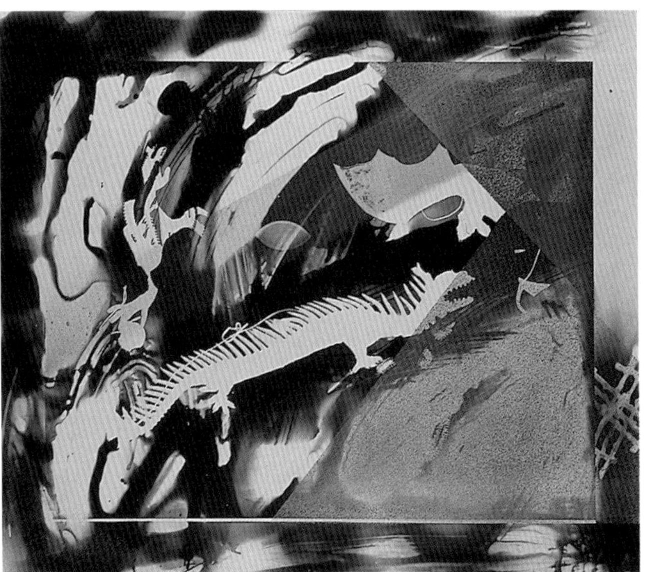

David Yager, from the series Lost Souls, 1992, silver gelatin print, hand-colored, 20x40 inches.

In 1968, I was invited to join the Art Faculty at UCLA where I taught for four years with Robert Heinecken, one of the earliest proponents of the use of appropriated imagery and certainly the leading West Coast non-traditionalist photo artist. I was invited to join the faculty of the Department of Art at Florida State University in 1972; I accepted that offer because I was impressed by the concepts and attitudes of the art faculty who were establishing a program in which all disciplines of studio art were treated equally in an interdisciplinary manner. This seemed consonant with my view of art as image making that transcends the limitations of any one medium.

I continue to view myself as an experimentalist, a narrative artist whose interest is in the expression of some of the questions raised by human existence.

## DAVID YAGER

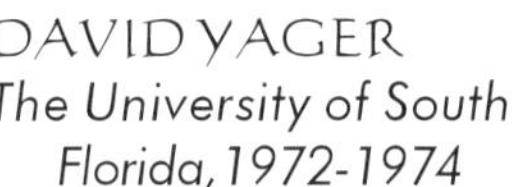

*The University of South Florida, 1972-1974*

When I was asked to start a graduate program in photography at Florida State University, I recruited David Yager and Fred Ensley to come as graduate students and serve as my first teaching assistants. Both Ensley (who had studied with me at UCLA) and Yager were close colleagues and they responded to my admonishment to push photography's boundaries.

Upon completion of his MFA, Yager was hired to teach at the University of South Florida, where he later became department chairman and then director of Graphicstudio. He left USF to become chairman of the Department of Art at the University of Maryland, Baltimore County, where he founded one of the leading graduate level computer graphics programs in the country, the Imaging Research Center. David Yager's early photographic vision was greatly influenced by the

Swiss photographer Robert Frank. He had been exposed to Frank's images while studying with Mike McLaughlin at the University of Connecticut and he liked the honesty of Frank's vision. Robert Frank's book, *The Americans*, influenced Yager's generation and established the field of street photography in America, setting up the arena for such photographers as Winogrand and Friedlander. Yager moved into photography from an early interest in creative writing; he realized that since words gave him visual images he could work with visual images directly. While at the University of Connecticut Yager was mentored by the poet James Scully, who in addition to supporting Yager's vision, gave him a book he had edited, *Poets on Poetry*; Yager read it in tandem with Nathan Lyons' collection of essays by photographers, *Photographers on Photography*. Yager points out that both books dealt with image making but that the poets were better able to articulate their ideas.

While his early influences were all single frame image makers, Yager very quickly began to explore layering of images through a variety of techniques, cutting and pasting, then rephotographing, multiple printing, etc. When he started teaching he felt that "a photograph should look like anything you think it should look like." Today he points out that "there's no such thing as photography... it's all just making marks on different surfaces... its all about collecting things and making marks... collecting images, collecting ideas, getting them down on paper in some way."

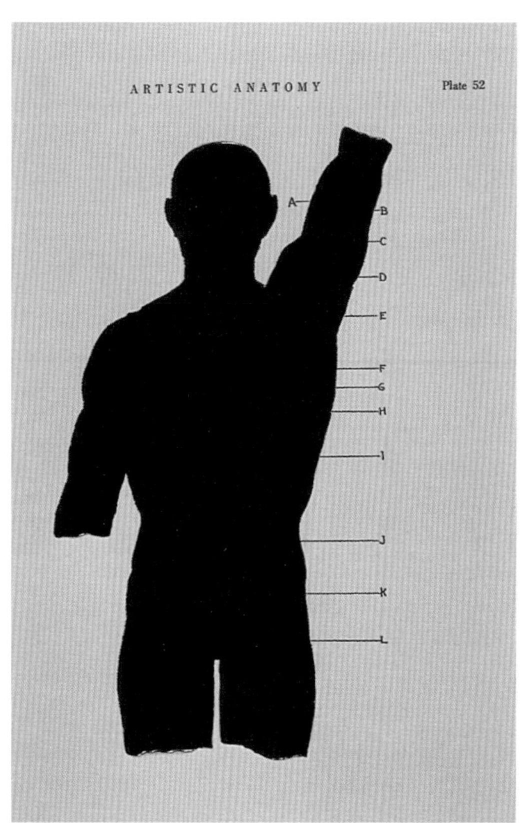

Tyler Turkle, *Artistic Anatomy, Plate 52*, 1985-89, 8½x12 inches each (seven pieces in total). Private Collection, Tallahassee, Florida.

## TYLER TURKLE
*Florida State University, 1975-1987*

When Tyler Turkle joined the faculty at Florida State University in 1975, his attitude was that photographic artists should be *making* not *taking* photographs. His photographic mentor was Richard Meyers, filmmaker, at Kent State University in Ohio. In his film work Tyler has followed the *cinema verité* documentary approach. His films include *Walk That Dog, The Rugby Film, Cut, Wakulla, The Last Days of Eddy Marconi* and *Gators, Wrestlers, Football Players* (a work in progress).

In his still image work Turkle laid out an approach on the experimental / appropriationist edge of photography. Working from projected slides of a Jerry's Restaurant placemat he poured *Mona Breakfast* (1976) onto a sheet of white velvet. Jerry's Restaurant, now long gone, featured the highest of kitsch decorations and ambience. This fascination with popular culture is intrinsic to Turkle's Plastic Publicity series of the 1980s, in which he poured plastic on publicity stills from commercial films. In these 8x10" images, the poured plastic is used to radically transform the publicity stills into silhouettes. They point in a direct way back to the nineteenth century tradition of silhouette portraiture. These create a radical subversion of the virtues of the continuous tone, lens formed image, taking everything out but the outline of the figures photographed and the positive/negative shapes of the picture plane. This reduction to a more primitive visual form thus leads us to see just how much of our perception is based on the outlines of objects. The ordinary and the mundane are removed; the essence remains. In more recent large scale images, Turkle uses a similar strategy with large scale color prints, but he plays large monochromatic shapes against lens formed information to create a tension between a generic color print and modernist art object.

## VIRGIL MIRANO

*Florida State University, 1976-1977*

Virgil Mirano loved the work of traditional West Coast photographers—Edward Weston, Minor White, Wynn Bullock—but he resisted emulating them when he began to make his own work. He questioned why he should redo that work. In a sense Mirano's work in this exhibition can be directly related to the work of the French artist Yves Klein, not only in form but in attitude; it reflects his desire to use the most direct means possible to express his feelings. His use of the found, the discarded and the human form as *signs* falls within the field of endeavor explored by Klein. Unlike Klein, Mirano did not have an art agenda; his pieces are in part a result of his habit of "rag picking," looking through the castoffs of an age of excessive image production. As he looked though the trash heap of a printing company, he began to appreciate the proof prints and printing mistakes he found there. He came across rolls of discarded diazo paper, a product that architects and engineers used to reproduce their drawings. This paper required ultraviolet light and thus could not be projected upon by any readily available means. It could however be used to make photograms. It was simply processed after exposure by ammonia fuming and it yielded a direct positive image. The long, wide strips of paper allowed Mirano to break free of the bounds of traditional form and scale. A figurative image maker to the core, he chose to contact print human beings and their clothing. He created the first of these large scale images while studying with Darrell Curran at California State University / Fullerton. The first time he showed his work, its scale and immediate impact attracted and entranced the other students, who came and stared in amazement. Mirano had used what was to him an ordinary everyday attitude of making something out of what was in front of him to create something new. The images were, as he points out, a product of the time, the late 1960s and early 1970s, in which everything was in play. For him there were no rules for art making. Mirano finished his degree at California State University / Fullerton and then completed his MFA at UCLA with Robert Heinecken, who had been Curran's mentor. He came to Florida State University for a year to fill in for me while I was away on leave. Mirano taught briefly at the Art Institute of Chicago and then returned to Los Angeles where he became deeply involved with motion picture production, especially the area of special effects. Recently he has become a highly valued cinematographer for filmmaker Victor Nunez and has won praise from film critic Gene Shalit, who has said that Mirano should have won an Academy Award for his work on the 1996 Nunez film *Ulee's Gold*, set in the Panhandle.

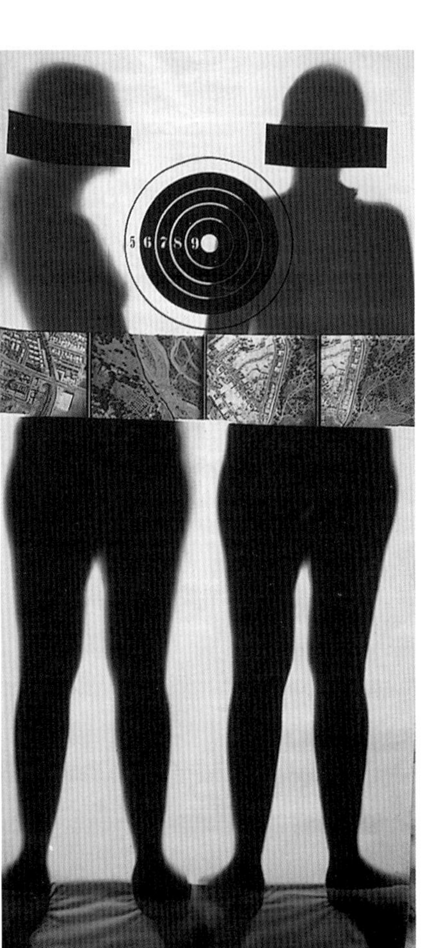

Virgil Mirano, *No Witness*, 1973, diazo paper with canvas backing, 82x36 inches.

## GEORGE BLAKELY
*Florida State University, 1978-present*

George Blakely studied with Darrell Curran, at California State University / Fullerton, for his undergraduate degree, and with William Larson, at Philadelphia's Tyler School of Art, for his master's degree. He is totally postmodernist in attitude toward the photographic image; even in his early student days he collected and assembled photographs. Blakely does not *make* photos, he *utilizes* them. Beginning in his undergraduate days while working at Disneyland, Blakely would collect the discarded Polaroids, the day's failed snapshots, and he would assemble them into various configurations. He then moved on to the myriad of photographs that are generated by the returned, rejected prints at photo finishing facilities. Of the resulting works, *Cubic Foot*, 1978, is the most radical. It is simply a cubic foot of reject prints bound and presented as a floor piece. It defeated all the preconceptions of photographic art form of the period. He continued more conventionally utilizing a grid, using various motifs: blue skies, dogs, etc. (*Delineation*, c. 1978, 20x25") and then moved on to making decorative, sculptural pieces with sets of postcards (*Florida Postcards*, 1981, 48x36"). He began to excise the photographic imagery from encyclopedias and photo history books to create a sort of subversive visual text (*Beaumont Newhall's History*, 1987, 6x8 feet). His reaction to the flood of photographic imagery led him to create a series of yard artworks in 1988. Setting rods of metal rebar into the earth outside his house he pushed issue after issue of popular magazines down toward the ground, creating stacks of magazines left to the elements, the ultimate anti-archival gesture. The City of Tallahassee was so upset by the sight of these pieces that they tried to force him to remove them from his yard. Blakley protested on the grounds of artistic license and good ecological recycling intentions and won. Today his yard is completely overgrown, with these sculptures competing with bamboo and native plants in riotous abundance. In recent years he has embedded his found images in plastic or cement rather than make flat work (*Tablets*, 1993-96). He is, however, currently attracted to transforming these cast pieces via computer scans into wall art (*We Clowns*, 1999).

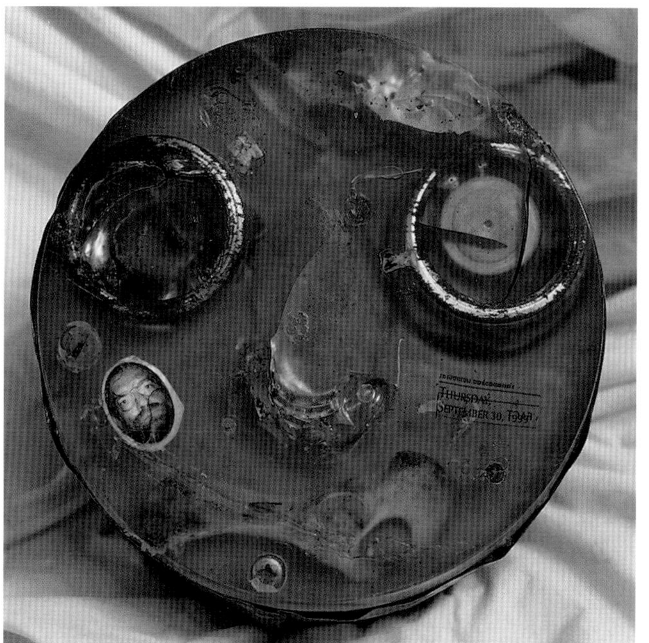

George Blakely, *We Clowns (9)*, 1999, inkjet print, mounted flush in grid, photo credit: George Bedell.

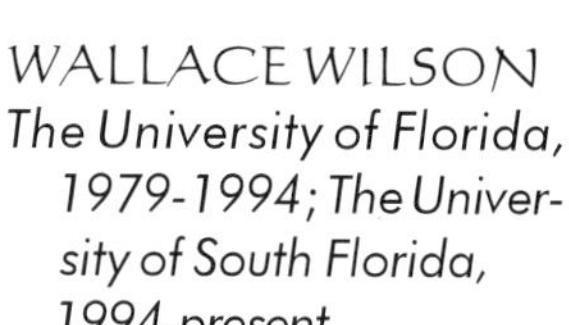

## WALLACE WILSON
*The University of Florida, 1979-1994; The University of South Florida, 1994-present*

When Wallace Wilson came to teach at the University of Florida, the demand for photography had continued at a striking rate. The photography program, with its stellar legacy of Uelsmann, Prince, Walker and Streetman, was a strong contender for national and international visibility.

Wilson notes that when he began teaching at the University of Kentucky in 1970, he would probably have said that a photograph was usually made with a camera and the print would be black and white, ranging in size from 4x6" to 11x14" and mounted on a white mat; by the time he was hired to join Uelsmann and Streetman he was highly involved in using collage. He soon added dimensionality in order to address the issue of the flatness of the photograph with a relief technique, augmented by hand coloring. By the mid-1980s, Wilson began to explore the issue of scale, an issue which has dogged photography over the years. He began to make large, black and white images (4x6 feet) of ordinary subjects from a visually disorienting perspective. He says, "I find gratification in the lack of specific (stable) answers to these images." For a work commissioned by the Southeast Museum of Photography in the late 1980s, Wilson created a gigantic image of a statue of a baby; it is on translucent material and appears to be "illuminated much like in a movie theater." He says of this work, "I wanted to see if the startling content and scale dominance of the singular image would carry a power to overwhelm the viewer. . .the picture of the baby statue truly became iconographic."

After teaching at The University of Florida for a decade and a half, Wallace Wilson accepted a position as chair of the Department of Art at the University of South Florida, where he remains at the present time.

Today Wilson holds the opinion that a photograph is simply a static lens formed image of some sort. He has begun to investigate digital imagery and its meaning for mass culture. He continues to explore large scale imagery; more recently these projects have greatly expanded in scale and involve other people interacting with him to create the work. He writes that: "one project involved text and pictures in a digitally printed 24x288" scroll that depicted the life of a senior citizen who lives in an assisted care facility. My 10 year-old daughter and her friends were the subjects—complete with period costumes and settings. My wife, Mary Straw, a teacher/ artist/designer, was my partner in the creation of the work."

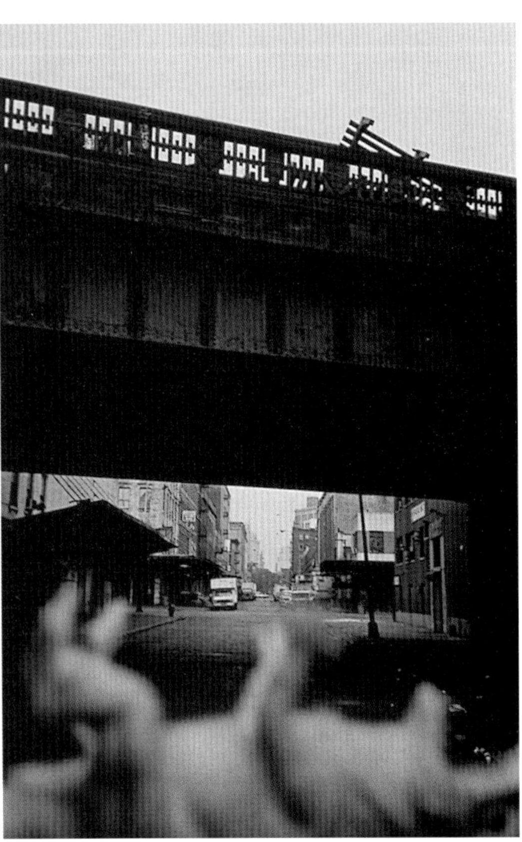

Wallace Wilson, *Urban Dinosaur*, 1988, silver gelatin print, 72x48 inches.

# AN INTERVIEW WITH VAN DEREN COKE

MUSEUM: Your professional colleagues think of your tenure at the University of Florida as the first established beachhead in the advancement of fine-art photography in the state of Florida. What was it like—was it difficult to get the medium accepted and taught?

Van Deren Coke: I hate to disappoint you, but it was not a pitched battle, at all. In fact, it couldn't have been easier. Clinton Adams was the Chairman of the Art Department at the time, and I was encouraged by him to take a position at UF. When I went to Gainesville, the problems were minimal; the only ones I remember were those associated with setting up a new program virtually overnight. I've heard that other colleagues had significant trouble with their programs, but that was never the case with my program. I used slides of paintings the first semester to teach the history of photography. The biggest change was moving out an instructor who had been teaching photography with a journalistic viewpoint to my approach, which was using photography as a means of conceptualizing one's ideas. In other words, using the medium to probe your imagination about life and much else.

MUSEUM: You have also been known as the first empire-builder—since you brought in Jerry Uelsmann as part of your legacy at UF and he has continued to work there throughout his career.

VDC: Photography was popular with the students. Classes were over-subscribed, so I felt the need of another teacher. To build the program, I consulted with a colleague I trusted, that was Henry Smith at Indiana University. He gave me two recommendations, one of whom was a recent MFA whose focus was fairly traditional. His second recommendation—I remember he said something like "Jerry's a wizard in the darkroom," which caught my attention because I wanted to open up the study of photography to see if the students could seek new directions. So I brought Uelsmann down to Florida.

MUSEUM: Did you know that we inquired about two of your works from Princeton's Art Museum for the exhibition here?

VDC: I know Peter Bunnell well, but didn't know Princeton had any of my prints. What does he have?

MUSEUM: Two discrete pieces, but actually, it's three works: two of the prints are mounted on a single board, a front and a back. They were both done in 1961; one title is *U.S. Highway 441* and the other is *Car Crushed Snake*.

VDC: Oh! He has *memento mori* pieces.

MUSEUM: You'd still find a lot of material for that down here—road-kill is abundant.

VDC: I was very interested in art that incorporated the concept of *memento mori* (death is always with us), a reminder of the transitory nature of life. I lectured on art as well as photography on this subject.

MUSEUM: Princeton also has *In Edward Weston's Garden*, 1955, a portrait of Ruth Bernhard.

---

*[The Interview was conducted by Allys Palladino-Craig in different segments in February and June of 2000 utilizing questions prepared by Robert W. Fichter.]*

VDC: I know that very interesting photograph. It has a history. Ruth Bernhard and I went in 1955 to visit Edward, who was failing. She had then and has to this day a reverential respect as well as love for this man and his work. After the visit, when we were leaving, she took a little spade and carefully dug up a small blossoming plant, dampening it down, so it would get all the way back to San Francisco. I talked to her recently. She said after all these years she's kept it growing and she said she was sending me a cutting, to keep the memory alive. The shot I took is probably the most romantic photograph in the entire history of American photography.

MUSEUM: Did you know Peter Bunnell back then?

VDC: Yes. When he came along, you could count on one hand the number of people seriously involved in the history of photography. He had taken Newhall's history of photography class at RIT. After graduating from that school, he went to Ohio University—the first school in America to offer a graduate degree in photography. But there were very few around teaching the history. There he met the head of the photography program, Clarence White's son. Peter became very interested in Clarence White, Sr., who was closely involved with Stieglitz. Peter is now a specialist on Clarence White's photographs.

MUSEUM: What about your own course of study? You said you went to grad school as an older student—could you elaborate on that?

VDC: After WWII, I went home to Kentucky. My family had had a wholesale hardware business for three generations, back to the nineteenth century. I was an only son so I went to work there, but I could see that everything was going to move faster now that the war was over. I wrote a little for a hardware trade journal about what I had learned from my experience as a naval officer in the war regarding the handling of large quantities of heavy things, ammunition and gear for mine sweepers.

MUSEUM: For example?

VDC: In the 5000 ton LSTs like I served on as Captain, we had forklifts that could lift large crates and store them in another part of the ship very quickly and unload them off of shelves high in the ship. I wrote one article urging the use of the new technology and new ways of thinking about how to cut costs in the wholesale hardware business. I could see that the old structure, paying minority laborers fifty cents an hour to lift refrigerators and other heavy things was on the way out, and I soon saw that the way business was being done, both in terms of the labor force and in terms of small mom-and-pop stores in every community—there would be changes in the distribution of goods and other changes as cars and roads got to the point that retail customers could shop around, and go to urban areas for greater selection. I knew my family business, as a concept, was on the way out and I did not relish the responsibilities involved with making major changes. I wanted to go to graduate school to be an art historian.

MUSEUM: How did you know what you wanted to study?

VDC: I'd been researching various topics for articles in the arts and history section of the Louisville *Courier Journal*. I wrote what interested me, because that was my educational background, history and English. One article I wrote was posing the question about how the very first daguerreotype made in Kentucky had come about in 1840 a few months later than it was initially introduced to the world in Paris.

MUSEUM: How did you pick Indiana University?

VDC: I was introduced to Dr. Henry Hope at College Art Association meetings. I would go to CAA meetings with the faculty members of the University of Kentucky who had been my teachers when I was an undergraduate. They gave me entrée to the meetings. I was still with my family's business when Henry Hope encouraged me to come to IU. Since I would be returning as an older student in the post-war atmosphere, he said I'd have to work twice as hard as other grad students, meaning the younger grad students, but that did not stop me. He also cautioned me, once I was there, that I must stick with the art history faculty and not have anything to do with the history of photography course being taught by Henry Smith. Smith was the first person in the States—and therefore in the world—to give a university course on the history of photography as an art form. Actually, I had known Smith even before I was introduced to Dr. Hope. Smith used to organize seminars, not necessarily even connected with the university, and I took Meatyard along to one of them.

MUSEUM: But you turned to the dark side and took your MFA instead in sculpture rather than a graduate degree in art history.

VDC: I presented my idea for my Master's thesis to a panel of art historians, Dr. Hope at the head, and I said I wanted to deal with the idea that nineteenth-century photography had a *serious* influence on nineteenth-century painting. Great silence. Hope asked me to leave the room. When I came back, he suggested that a paper I'd already written on an American landscape artist, George Inness, would be what I would—or should—expand for my thesis. In other words, forget the photo angle. I had become a friend of Professor Robert Laurent, the professor of sculpture. I told him what had happened in my meeting with the art historians. He knew I had done some sculpture in Mexico and asked to see photos. My wife back in Lexington dug some out and sent them to me. Laurent looked at them and said I should come to Ogunquit, Maine, where he had a summer school for advanced students. I did this and created a number of pieces in various kinds of materials. Then he suggested I go with him to the American Academy in Rome as an assistant.

MUSEUM: And who could blame you. You didn't stay too long in Rome, though.

VDC: Five months later I got a cable from Professor Clinton Adams, the Chairman of the Art Department at UF. He said I should come teach in Gainesville—the history of modern art—and set up a photography program.

MUSEUM: He is the reason you were at the University of New Mexico, too?

VDC: Adams was called from Gainesville to set up Tamarind Institute in Los Angeles, its first location. After that he took the position of Dean of the College of Fine Arts at UNM and called me again to be the founding director of UNM's new art museum. I went to UNM as a professor in the Department of Art and taught a seminar each semester. Dean Adams and the Chairman of the Department of Art had a serious disagreement about the future of the Department. The Chairman subsequently accepted a similar position elsewhere and I became both Chairman of the Department of Art and Director of the new art museum.

MUSEUM: Your research has covered the use of the photograph by artists—an iconoclastic idea when you first proposed it.

VDC: I've always been a rather independent thinker, and when I returned to school as an older student, I had the confidence to explore issues on my own. I don't follow the party line. I researched my theory that a great deal of the "art" from 1839 to the present was based in part on photographs. Artists are among the first to adapt new things for their own use. I just couldn't understand why so few academics, the art historians, couldn't see that. But I guess if your experience is limited to research in books and you don't know how an artist solves problems because you've never stepped into an artist's studio, you have trouble seeing what they are doing. I practically had to fight a whole war myself trying to get historians and critics to just *look*, and stop believing that most artists were purists, referring largely to previous art. Artists are resourceful—they scavenge, they range far and wide for new ideas, they like new technology. They take what they need. Photography is terribly attractive to them for it opens up new avenues.

MUSEUM: At Indiana University, your mentor was the head of the Art Department. By the time Robert Fichter was at IU, there was an obvious rivalry between the aristocratic Hope and the working class ideals of Henry Holmes Smith who championed the lowly form of photography as a radical new art form based on his work with Moholy-Nagy in Chicago.

VDC: Dr. Hope was not a high and mighty person, he was quite open, but he served both the university and even the international community. A world traveler, he was involved with projects at the United Nations. He was often away, or called away suddenly, and because I was older and could lecture, he would ask me to fill in for him for a lecture which he could not deliver because he was away from campus. I would go into the slide room all night and select slides, for instance on Matisse, that I knew something about and lecture the next day. It was a kind of trial by fire.

Henry Smith was a hard worker with a Bachelor degree in journalism, from Ohio State as I recall. He was a thinker, saw the possibilities in a whole new way of conveying ideas through photographic images. This was not something Hope paid much attention to. Smith was drafted to work for Hope on the College Art Association Bulletin. He worked on everything from providing pictures to editing and writing copy because of his background in journalism. Hope was the Editor and he and Smith had different styles of life, but Hope was a very busy man and a leader in the College Art Association and in the training of art historians so Henry Smith did some of Hope's work outside of IU class responsibilities.

MUSEUM: You mentioned Ralph Eugene Meatyard. Robert Fichter says he practiced photography the same way many American poets have written poetry—as a means of personal expression.

VDC: He was very well read, a friend of the poet Thomas Mertin and distinguished members of the University of Kentucky English Department. He had a business, an optician shop, but he was dedicated to creative photography and made a gallery on one side of his office to show his pictures as well as photographs by other adventurous photographers.

MUSEUM: We've been talking steadily about photography, but a little while back, you explained how you'd ended up with a degree in Sculpture. How did you get from point A to point B?

VDC: Through the interest in me voiced by the French sculptor Robert Laurent. Laurent thought the PhDs had little vision when confronted with new concepts. He thought it was a silly prohibition to drop a topic like I proposed, but I had a career-clock ticking and it was time to be on my way, so when Laurent offered me a place in his grad program I took it. I traveled to Maine and worked with him for two summers and then to Rome (my wife and children, too) and became proficient in the technical aspects of bronze casting and learned a lot as his assistant on the large floating female figure he was creating for a fountain at IU. Around the basin in which the 'floated' figure was to be placed were fish spraying water on her. I did some of the preliminary work on the fish. Laurent knew many artists in Italy. He was at the core of the Rome artists' colony; and he knew important artists in New York and he collected American folk art. I met through him painters and sculptors which was an education in itself and looked in Brooklyn for antique folk art with him.

MUSEUM: Did you ever see much of Hope or Smith after leaving Indiana?

VDC: I saw quite a bit of Henry Smith, who had moved when he retired, to California, where I had become Director of the Department of Photography at the San Francisco Museum of Modern Art. Smith was always invited to the openings of the shows and we had good talks. He was very interested in my focus on German, French, and Czech photography from 1920 to the 1930s. Smith knew that modern photography had not come out of America, but was born in the Bauhaus. Moholy-Nagy, who was Jewish, came to Chicago from Germany when the Bauhaus was closed by Hitler. He set up a new school in Chicago. Smith met him there. I first learned about European photography and modern design by looking at Moholy's photographs in European magazines. Smith and Professor Raymond Barnhart, who taught at the University of Kentucky, had studied with Moholy in Chicago. Barnhart gave me the ideas of the genesis of modern photography. Henry Smith also told me about the concepts of this universal man Moholy-Nagy. Later at the SFMoMA, I decided to concentrate on not so well-known work of avant-garde European photographers. The director, Henry Hopkins knew that four or five other museums around the country had concentrated on American photography, so he was ready to help me build a collection we could acquire for little money at the time and which was truly innovative work—if we got to Europe before other curators did. I could always get what I needed to make museum purchases from my supporters backed up by Hopkins. The dealers learned I was on the prowl for European work and helped me meet people in Europe who would in turn introduce me to major 1920s and 1930s photographers or their families.

MUSEUM: Why did the California museums start by collecting American photography, instead of looking internationally?

VDC: Very few American or European photographers were being acquired by museums in the West. The stature of Adams and the 1930s avant-garde F-64 Group gave SFMoMA a head start for they had works by Weston and Adams, and Georgia O'Keeffe had given them prints she had by Stieglitz plus they had good examples of Lange and Cunningham and other major photographers who lived in the San Francisco Bay area. These were acquired before I arrived. Hopkins wanted to build an international museum and felt photography was one way to go. He was much impressed after one opening of a show of photographs that had recently been added to the collection. When it was exhibited on one side of the museum and a Motherwell show on the other, everybody stayed in the photography galleries. Hopkins decided we could corner the market on modern European photography for we were at least two years ahead of everybody else.

MUSEUM: The museum had no European photography?

VDC: Not in any programmatic sense. The Museum of Modern Art *was* acquiring some European photographs and Captain Steichen, who organized *The Family of Man,* had acquired for MoMA a lot of photographs for that wonderful show, much of which stayed at MoMA. His successor John Szarkowski had the idea that America was where it was all happening with Winogrand, Arbus, Friedlander and Callahan and the like, but he had done little European research. That's why San Francisco has such an outstanding collection of 1920-1935 European photography.

MUSEUM: As much as you looked at photography, though, you spent a lot of time looking at paintings.

VDC: Yes. I would have done so even if I were not intimately involved with painting—to keep up with day-to-day activities. This was especially true when I was researching the book and exhibition *The Painter and the Photograph*.

MUSEUM: *The Painter and the Photograph* was done before you went to SFMoMA?

VDC: Yes. Going back a little bit, I went to the University of New Mexico to start a new museum in 1962. While I was at UF, I spent my summers taking classes at Harvard. Sam Hunter of Brandeis University was one of my teachers at Harvard. He was Director of the Rose Art Museum and he helped immensely when it came to getting the loan of paintings in Europe for *The Painter and the Photograph* exhibition that traveled. On opening night at the Rose Art Museum, the well-regarded scholar Creighton Gilbert, who had left IU and become Chairman of the Brandeis University Department of Art, was present and congratulated me on the research I had done. He was one of the professors who earlier was unwilling to have me pursue the topic that I had made into a major book and exhibition. After leaving IU, I showed many people that Cézanne worked from photographs, Gauguin worked from photographs as did so very many more artists. I used to say I was going to write a book about the painters who *never* worked from photographs and that it would be a very thin volume, indeed. But my research carried a negative charge in the minds of most art historians and dealers. I was threatened with a lawsuit by the wife of Charles Sheeler who thought the value of his work would go down if his use of photographs were known. Sheeler had been making fine photographs for many years and using them as models for his paintings. I knew him and he showed them to me.

MUSEUM: How did you get where you are?

VDC: You mean in photography? I was interested in photography even when I was about fourteen at a boarding school, where there was a darkroom for the school paper and annual. I had access to it and did a good deal of photography for I was tackled from behind in a football game, which broke one of my legs and left me unusually free to roam on the large farm where the school was located because I could not participate much in sports. In 1937 in Lexington, Kentucky, a camera club was formed and an industrial chemist—Ben Hart who had retired, joined the club. He gave a course to ten or so of the members. They ranged from me, a teenager, to faculty members from the university. Hart would show us how to select certain photo papers for certain effects because he understood the chemistry of the process and the nature of different papers. At the end of class meetings at his home, he would show us Edward Weston prints in his collection, saying "this is what we aspire to."

MUSEUM: You met Weston?

VDC: I drove cross country to see him in 1938. My father's sister lived in Piedmont across from San Francisco, so I stayed with her for a day or so, then went down to Carmel to meet Weston. I took an inexpensive room in a little tourist motel and set out for Wildcat Hill. I knocked on his door and explained why I was there, he was very modest and invited me to come in. Weston started showing me his prints about which he didn't say much unless I asked him something specific. He asked me to come back a number of times. One day he took me to Point Lobos which was due west of his house. I carried his 8 x 10 camera and aluminum box of film. I watched what he was doing when he set up to photograph and talked to him about his choices of rocks and trees along the water's edge. He was busy printing negatives from his second Guggenheim award so he was sometimes unavailable. I used the time I did not see him to understand better what he was doing. I felt the metamorphosis of the actual object before him was made to stand for many other things. I'd look at what he'd taken as subjects and finally I got it in my mind that it was a kind of spiritual transformation that he sought. Weston was very generous with his time so I asked him if he would take me on as a student. He told me to go see Ansel Adams, who was more the teacher, he said. I did meet Adams for the first time on that trip, but it wasn't until after the war, as a grown man, that I stayed a few weeks with the Adams family in Yosemite and was a student of his. I had a warm relationship with Ansel as an artist, even though his work did not play a role in the direction of my own interests.

MUSEUM: Since you've had multiple careers—professor, artist, museum professional—I wonder about the intersection of those insights, where the critical faculty of teaching and creating merges in the role of curator. How many photography exhibitions have you curated?

VDC: Well over fifty.

MUSEUM: And of which ones are you most proud?

VDC: Three come to mind that I did at The San Francisco Museum of Modern Art. They are, *Avant-Garde Photography in Germany, 1919-1939* and the first one-man show of the work of Joel-Peter Witkin, who had been one of my strongest graduate students at UNM. The exhibition catalogue/book on German photography was printed in German, French and Italian. I understand the catalogue for the Witkin show has gone into the third or fourth printing for SFMoMA. Of course, we had to talk to the press early on for Witkin's show because of the imagery, but there were no problems like some shows of Mapplethorpe's work provoked. With the help of Diana C. DuPont I researched and wrote about what I felt were some of the strongest photographs acquired for SFMoMA in the late 1970s and the early 1980s. One hundred and forty-one photographs were reproduced, many of them never published before in the USA. *Photography, A Facet of Modernism* was the title of the exhibition and book. I was especially pleased with the response to this book.

MUSEUM: Go back a second: so with Witkin you posted those 'viewer discretion' signs?

VDC: Any reasonable museum has to prepare its visitors so they can better understand what an artist is doing. The Witkin exhibition was enormously popular.

MUSEUM: Did a response to the medium play a part in that?

VDC: Possibly, but the response to the artist's imagination and high level of craftsmanship was much in evidence in the reviews.

MUSEUM: Different media have lifespans—times in which the work being done is new and artists flock to experiment themselves, based on what they saw another artist doing.

VDC: I saw this in San Francisco, but I also saw painters co-opting photography, so they could produce bigger images, images that didn't have to be sharp or truly "realistic," but they wanted incorporated in their imagery.

MUSEUM: Robert Fichter asked about what made photography so intriguing to a generation of American painters in the sixties and seventies.

VDC: It was because photography opened up new visual avenues which created a sense of liberation from stock subjects. A new generation were fascinated by *Life*, *Look* and other weekly photo magazines. These weekly publications used photography in extraordinarily different ways. Then there was Warhol and those things Hockney did with photos he had processed by a drugstore. They weren't anything like the photographs of Adams or Friedlander. Hockney enlarged the scale of photographs as well as created a kind of Cubist image that was amusing and many-faceted.

MUSEUM: You mean like the work of Virgil Mirano in this exhibition—a California artist now in the film industry?

VDC: Yes, or like the media experiments of another artist whose exhibition I was proud to have curated—Val Telberg. He was a Swedish-Russian intellectual, trained as a chemist, who was bored to death by doing chemistry for a New Jersey paint factory. He turned to amateur cinematography and later turned to buying out-of-date boxes of photosensitive paper which he used as a matrix for things he would like to have created in films. The combining of negatives and positives was a limiting technique, but he did extraordinary work with his ideas. Presentation for him was just a matter of thumb-tacking his images to the wall—which was unheard of in serious photography circles.

MUSEUM: That's a cheery prospect—shipping bills for an exhibition limited to tubes of rolled up paper—no crates, no frames, virtually no cost!

VDC: Not what we'd call archival because the images can fade and get brittle. Great conceptually, wonderful to look at, unstable.

MUSEUM: Permanence didn't seem to be a concern, not like it was with the artists who were working when you were just establishing your career.

VDC: Altogether different approach.

MUSEUM: What about your work, your thoughts? Was it, as the critic Thomas Barrow has said of your 1970s work, that you were overwhelmed by Weston?—that you had seen what Weston had done in straight photography and didn't choose to follow in his footsteps, but instead turned in a different direction to stake out new claims? Robert Fichter discusses the "flashing" of your photographs—the muting and transmuting of tones, and the reversal of naturalistic lighting—he is also aware that you met Man Ray in Paris in 1960 and that that may also have had an influence.

VDC: Actually, it was not Weston's shadow, but Man Ray's innovative ways of using photography that influenced me. I have always had the greatest of respect for Weston, as did all of us, but I don't feel there's anything I could do that could be put alongside one of his prints. Man Ray showed me a good cross section of his Rayographs and Surreal photographs and I began working in a similar fashion.

MUSEUM: You traveled to Paris to meet artists like Man Ray?

VDC: No. I wasn't the novitiate I had been on my pilgrimage to Weston. I met Man Ray in Paris at a party, as I recall it was at one of Virginia Zabriskie's affairs. She was the first dealer who ventured to sell modern twentieth-century photography in Paris. She deserves a lot of credit being an American who showed very interesting European and American photographs. I saw work in Paris after WWII all the time that was worthy of being shown and collected yet was little known in the United States. I liked Paris for you'd never hear a painter talking about the act of painting as an art event, or how one put paint on a brush—no, they talked about concepts and deeper issues, There was still a strong vein of pre-WWII Surrealism which I found challenging. What I saw and heard influenced me just as some of the 1930s works done in Germany had opened up my eyes.

MUSEUM: We think it's interesting who great artists' heroes are.

VDC: Many of my insights came from teaching art history. I was teaching the history of modern art when I met Man Ray, whose paintings did not get much attention in the 1960s, but which I found to be fascinating. He supported himself largely with fashion photography (he said *Vogue* always picked the wrong pictures). His paintings and some of his photographs were Surreal, although not Surreal enough to get him very far in the art world. My work certainly wasn't in emulation of Man Ray's, for he solarized negatives from which he made prints. I "flashed" my prints while in the developer, therefore each print is unique. I had about a ten-second window to make up my mind about when to remove a print from the developer and get it in double-hypo to arrest the image's development, that is at a stage I wanted to be preserved for the prints turned black in a few seconds if I didn't get them in hypo immediately. Man Ray and a number of others were making solarized images in the 1920s. Moholy-Nagy solarized negatives not so much to make fine prints but as experiments. My process was mutable, the images I saw were fugitive, until I stopped the process by putting it quickly in hypo. The state I captured resulted in a kind of *monoprint*.

MUSEUM: You were looking for certain abstract qualities—formal qualities—as you manipulated the print in the darkroom?

VDC: There's a certain kind of detachment about my imagery but the photographic quality comes through many times. A blown-up portion of negative could change from being a sharp focus into something softer and not so "real." When I switched to color it was because I was very busy in San Francisco at SFMoMA and for the first time in my life I did not have a darkroom. I relied on a technician in Berkeley who could do very well what I asked him to do. My Mexican subject matter was made up of a good deal of contrast between colors and black which was important and appropriate for that combination I saw much of in Mexico.

MUSEUM: Let's go back to when you taught Meatyard when

you were involved with the Lexington Camera Club. According to Robert Fichter, he, Jerry Uelsmann, and Wally Wilson were all influenced by this rather unassuming artist.

VDC: It's true I was Gene's mentor for awhile, but all artists get beyond that state if they develop a special vision. He had an individual spirit. He wasn't making pictures to sell. I used to look at his work a lot, but he rarely said anything even after I made a comment about a print. His best things were surreal, more poetic, more dreamlike than anyone I knew. I never really thought that he belonged in the Surreal (capital) category. He was unique. In New Orleans, Clarence John Laughlin was somewhat like Gene. Clarence had a library full of strange, archaic and mysterious literature. He was literary-minded, as was Gene to a certain extent. Gene wasn't at all like Uelsmann. Jerry has built a career out of making images through a process that is all his own. He has an amazing ability to choreograph intricate maneuvers in his darkroom in order to produce his complicated imagery. Gene did not orchestrate his imagery in the darkroom but with his eyes out in the open. Remember he died young; cancer of the esophagus so we can never know how far he could have developed his ideas. I think back fondly to the masks series he did. How inventive it was, how he made all of us a part of his special world. He started with his own children wearing masks at parties, then created a strange extended family that preserved us as members of his adult family. His wife was "Lucy Belle Crater," her mask name. It fit in with his sense of Gothic southern imagery, and even though he was from Illinois, he flourished in the atmospheric south he half-dreamed about, half-found around him.

MUSEUM: We have a quote from you: "Straight photography seems to have run out of ideas, that is serious ideas." Would you let me play devil's advocate and ask you if it is really the ideas that have been exhausted—or is it the evaporation of poetic insight as Fichter suggests?

VDC: Photography was wide open for a long time because there was no sustaining market for prints. Photographs were so full—so full of information—you could recognize who they admired and it was a closed-end situation no matter how poetic your temperament might have been unless you were a Meatyard. The photojournalists gave us one kind of information, then there were those who went far beyond 1930s FSA photographs. The leaders were Winogrand, Arbus, Friedlander plus Callahan to a degree. Weegee (Arthur Fellig) was much greater than people thought until recently. After awhile, the new photographers needed a different direction because they were beginning to run out of steam when it came to photographing people—so many of them went back to pretty pictures in color. For example, twenty years ago Uelsmann's work was far out at the edge, but he's been successful and success means followers (weak followers). It seems to me that serious photography is in a holding pattern. I feel that the teaching of photography in the universities has gotten tied to the way materials are used. A silver print is a silver print, and turning to platinum is not a forward step. The chemistry isn't changing much which is a limitation unto itself. Why have so few photographers worked with emulsion painted onto canvas? A few digital-made pictures are interesting as are the IRIS prints, but they only rarely end up used for a new kind of vision.

Recently, I went to a show of work by one of UNM's graduate students who has just been awarded a Guggenheim Fellowship. The work was autobiographical, big wax-coated images, sort of Lartique-like subjects. He is in all of them—really wonderfully weird, and the images link him to Meatyard. Hopefully, his ideas have "legs" and can be extended.

MUSEUM: So we have to pray for rain like the end of T.S. Eliot's *Wasteland*...think we'll get it?

VDC: My crystal ball is a little cloudy, right now.

*While I have juggled a handful of careers throughout most of my life, I have always tried to integrate my work so each part complemented the other. For example, my academic speciality is art history. Studying and teaching it for many years helped me to identify and develop the direction I wanted my own creative work to take. . . .I have always been as interested in teaching as in photographing. I wanted students to be made aware of the vast possibilities photography offers but it is not necessary for them to try to do everything. I encouraged them to explore in their own ways. In a university situation if you are very careful when picking graduate students you get a good mix of broad art backgrounds and technical knowledge. Following this premise I found pretty soon that graduate students teach each other. The primary role of the faculty is to keep the students excited and productive. I found one could learn all the requisite techniques of photography in a very short time. What is important is to stimulate ideas and provide a student with challenging responses and to provide a forum where advanced students are called to engage in a contest with each other—and I do not mean only graduate students in photography, but those in other fields. One danger is that we tend to intellectualize photography in many university programs. This takes the freshness out of someone who comes along and just wants to do his or her own thing, but without continuous discourse students can become so narrow-minded that they will not be successful teachers and my aim has been largely to train university teachers, for I do not know how to train "artists."*

*Constant exposure to students with new ideas has stimulated me to grasp what an individual is up to and offer suggestions about what to look at or read to foster his or her development. Students keep your blood flowing because you are also challenged to explain your comments. There is a danger in being totally involved with teaching for you pour your good ideas into the students, often exhausting yourself. You must feel that teaching is as important as your own creative art or you should find some other way of making a living. There is a feeling of being a missionary when you teach and counsel students. When they are productive, and even famous, you feel satisfied, as if they are relatives. That aspect of teaching keeps challenging you as new generations come along.*

*The photographer who knows how to analyze the language of his medium, often enriches it. It is that a photographer who has a way of reflecting upon past accomplishments of others and who absorbs them little by little can stake out his or her own terrain. After having known some of the masters I have been stimulated in two directions, and I have sought to integrate one with the other: the use of photography as a medium for exploring responses to life and not to overlook the history of art and photography. In my book* The Painter and the Photograph, *I sought to cast light on the extensive use painters have made of photography in their work. It is no longer the external reality that stimulates me, but the problem of evoking my inner responses to life and the world at large without being burdened by the way a camera records surface reality. By writing about teaching and collecting photographs I have been sensitized to the work of the most venturesome artists who have used photography. The dimension of time past played a role in my photography in the 1950s through the 1960s. I have used a found photograph or an old negative which connects my work with reality but not straightforward reality. I have often marked a print with my hand. This has had different meanings. I "borrowed" a photoprint of an aspect of the Vietnam War that had a portion of a picture integrated with a photograph of my hand in the traditional "stop" sign. Such a photograph becomes an image that reflects my philosophical position. This kind of image is temporal as well as an aesthetic image, belonging solely to the author.*

*At the present, with Fujicolor-Super HQ I began to photograph little things on the streets that seemed to have been created just for me. Looking down became more interesting than looking out at the world. Perhaps living in New Mexico where there are marvelous petroglyphs, created by the Indians for over 5000 years, influenced one of my current directions.*

**—Van Deren Coke**

OSCAR BAILEY

GEORGE BLAKELY

VAN DEREN COKE

ROBERT W. FICHTER

VIRGIL MIRANO

DOUG PRINCE

EVON STREETMAN

TYLER TURKLE

JERRY UELSMANN

TODD WALKER

WALLACE WILSON

DAVID YAGER

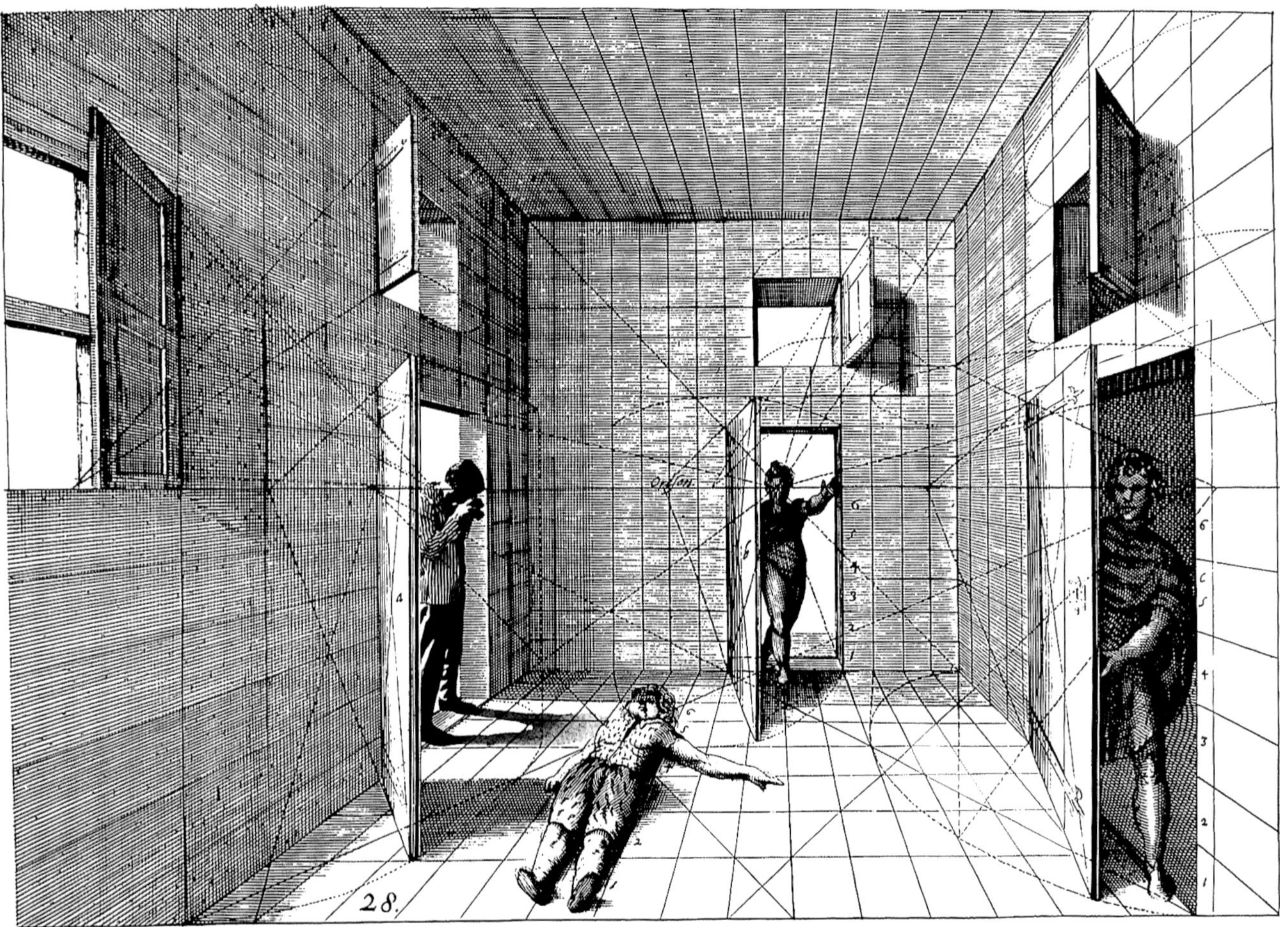

Oscar Bailey, *The Room*, 1972, cut, paste, and re-photograph, 15½x10½ inches.

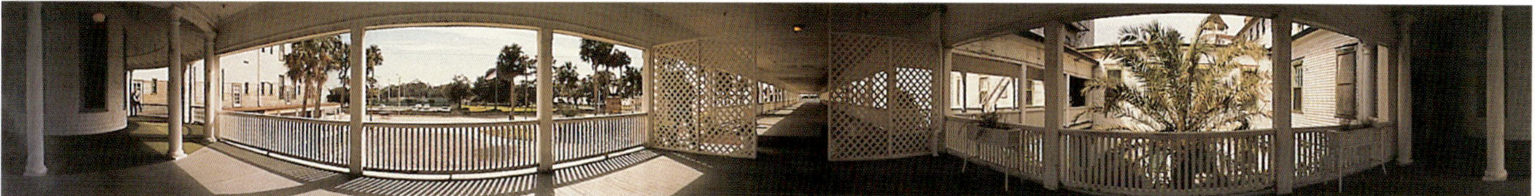

Oscar Bailey, *Oscar and Sara at the Ormond Beach Hotel, FL*, 1987, cirkut, 8x59 inches.

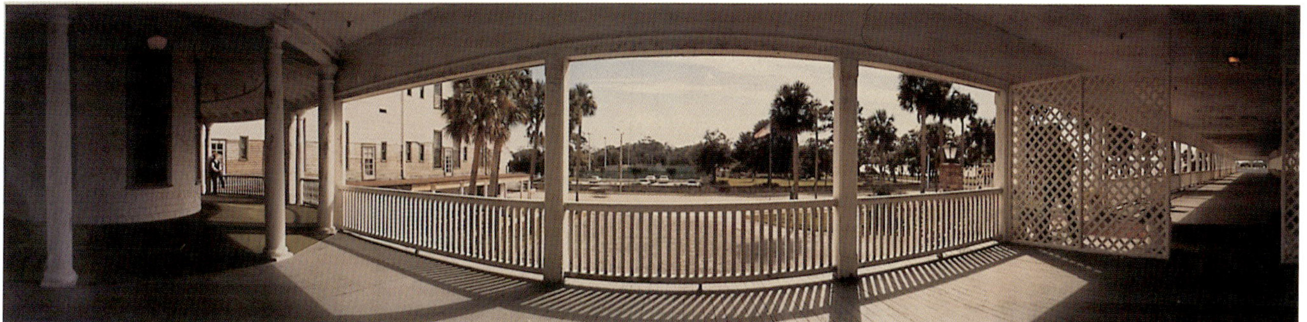

Oscar Bailey, [left detail] *Oscar and Sara at the Ormond Beach Hotel, FL*, 1987, cirkut.

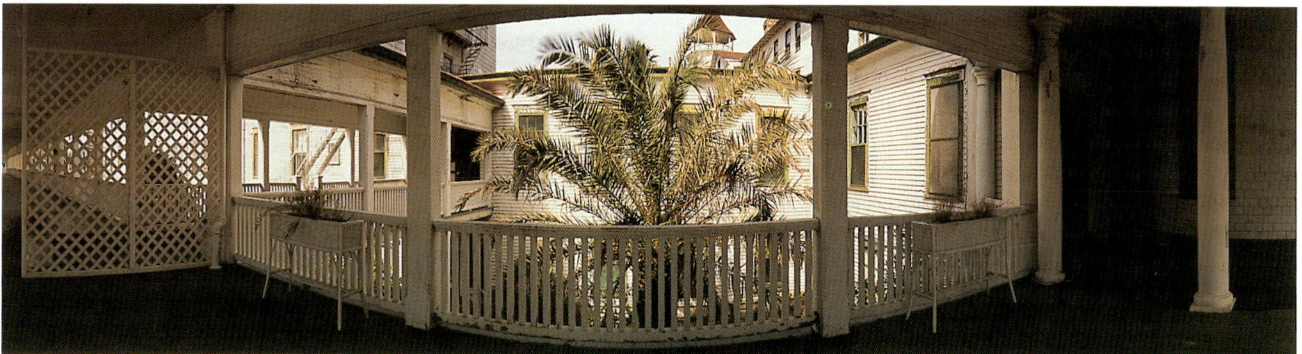

Oscar Bailey, [right detail] *Oscar and Sara at the Ormond Beach Hotel, FL*, 1987, cirkut.

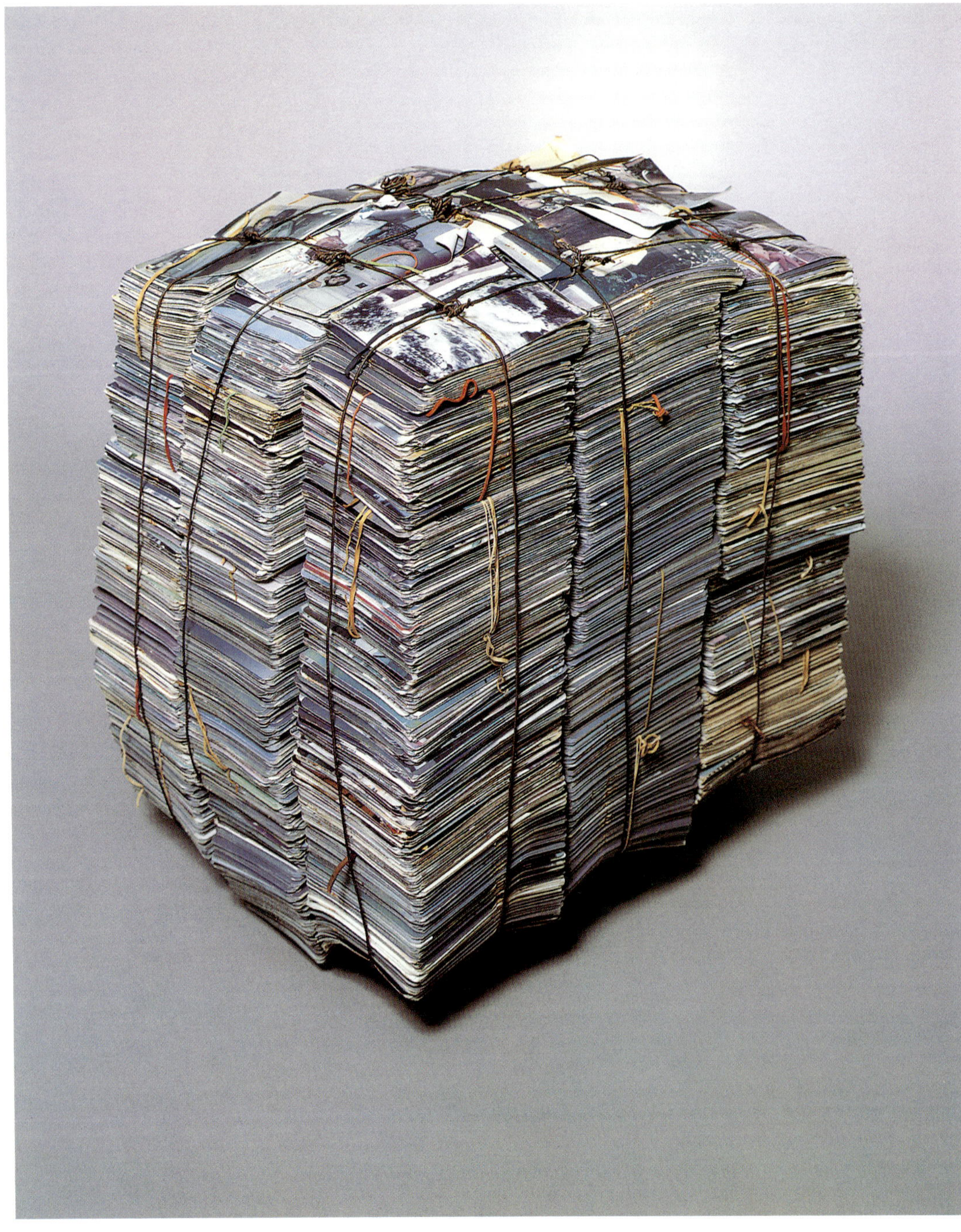

George Blakely, *A Cubic Foot of Photographs*, 1978, wire-bound photographs, c. one foot square each side (one cubic foot).

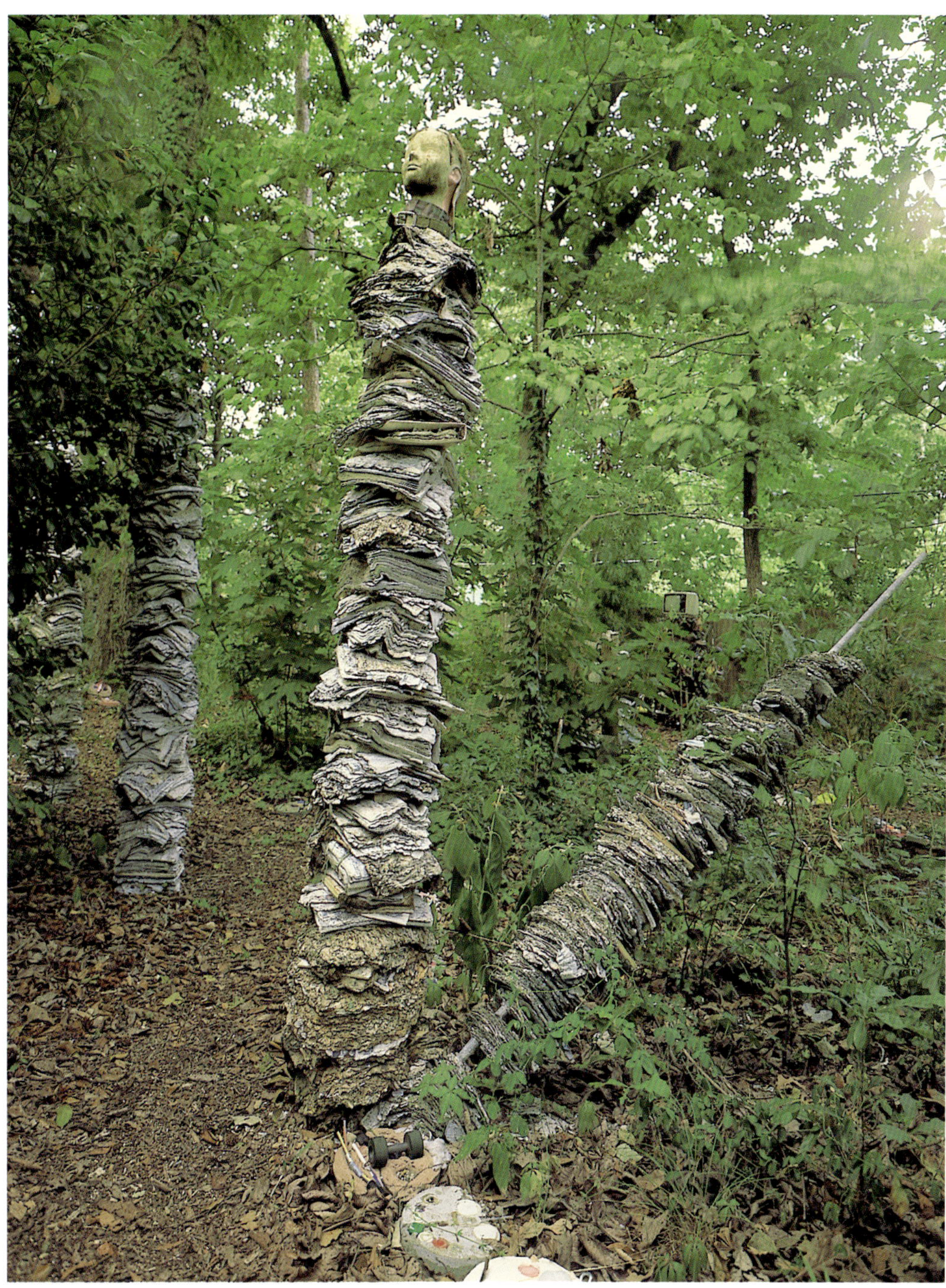

George Blakely, *Poles*, 1988-ongoing, *in situ* installation, dimensions variable, photo credit: George Bedell.

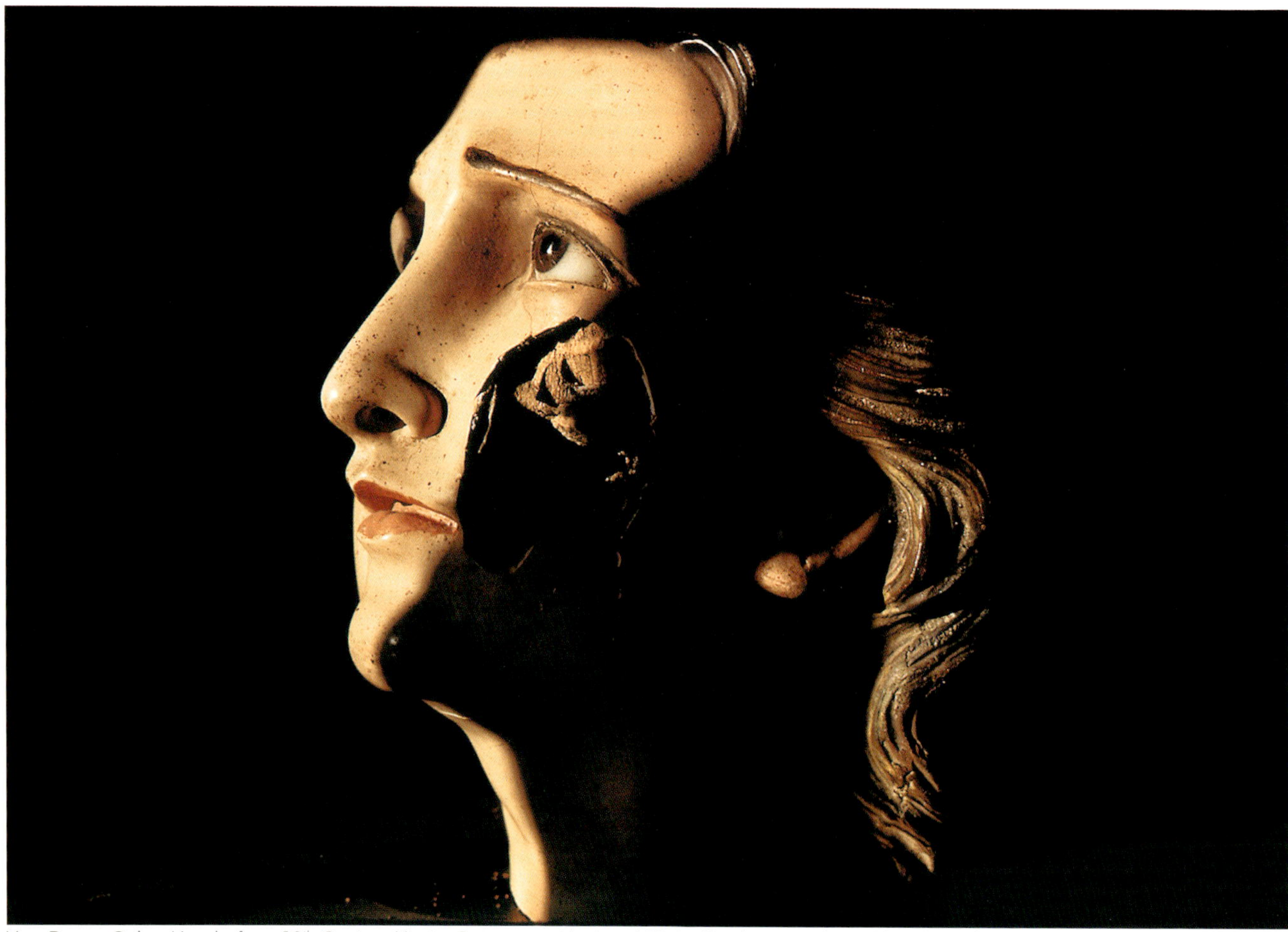

Van Deren Coke, *Head of an 18th Century Virgin, Patzcuaro, Mexico*, 1984, cibachrome print, 9¾x13¾ inches.

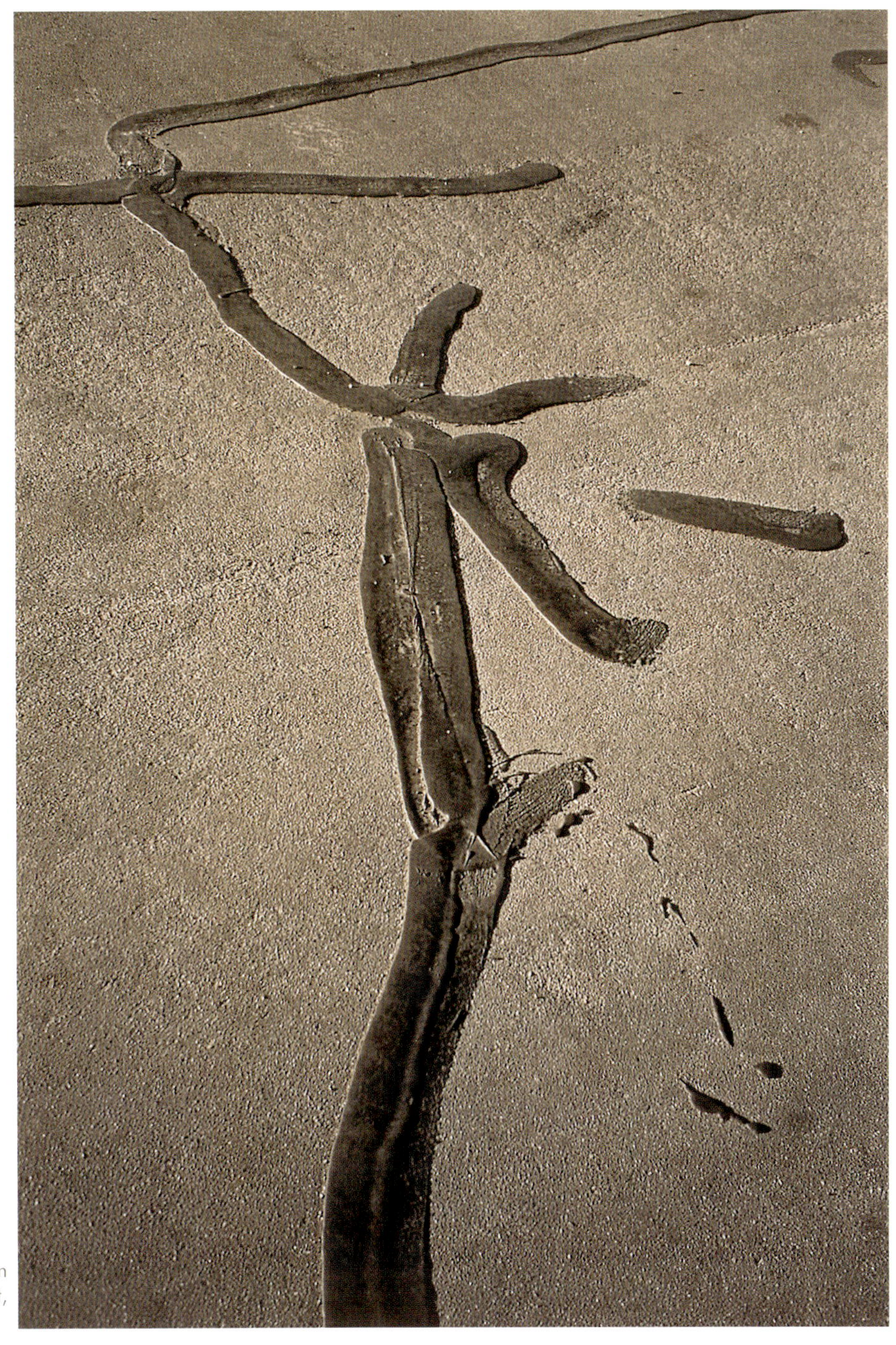

Van Deren Coke, *Wounded Warrior,* from *Looking Down* Series, 1999, Type C print, 13½x9⅓ inches.

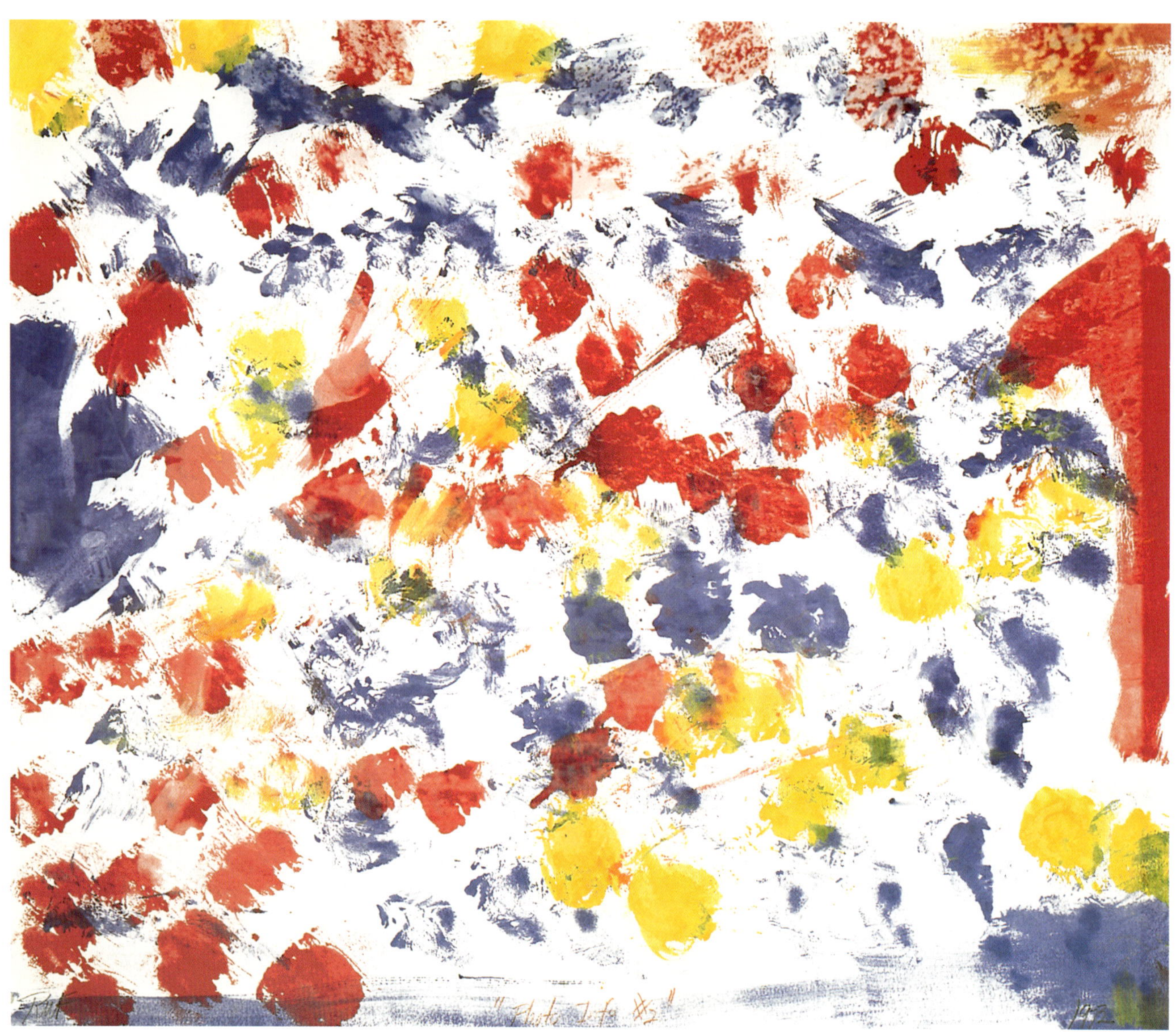

Robert W. Fichter, *Photo Info #2*, 1972, Inko dye, 23x19 inches.

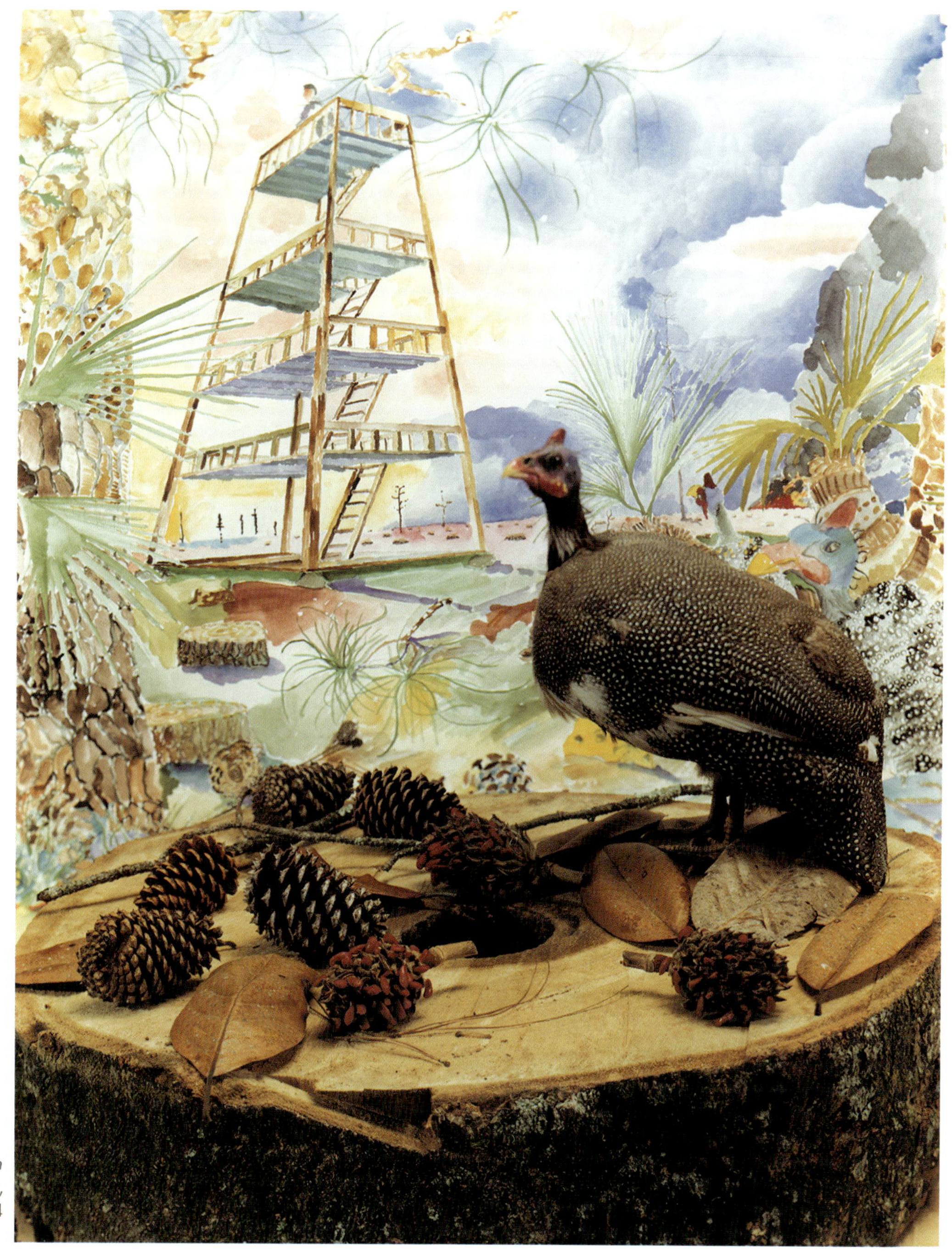

Robert W. Fichter, *Southern View #1: Forest Management*, 1999, Type C print, 20x24 inches.

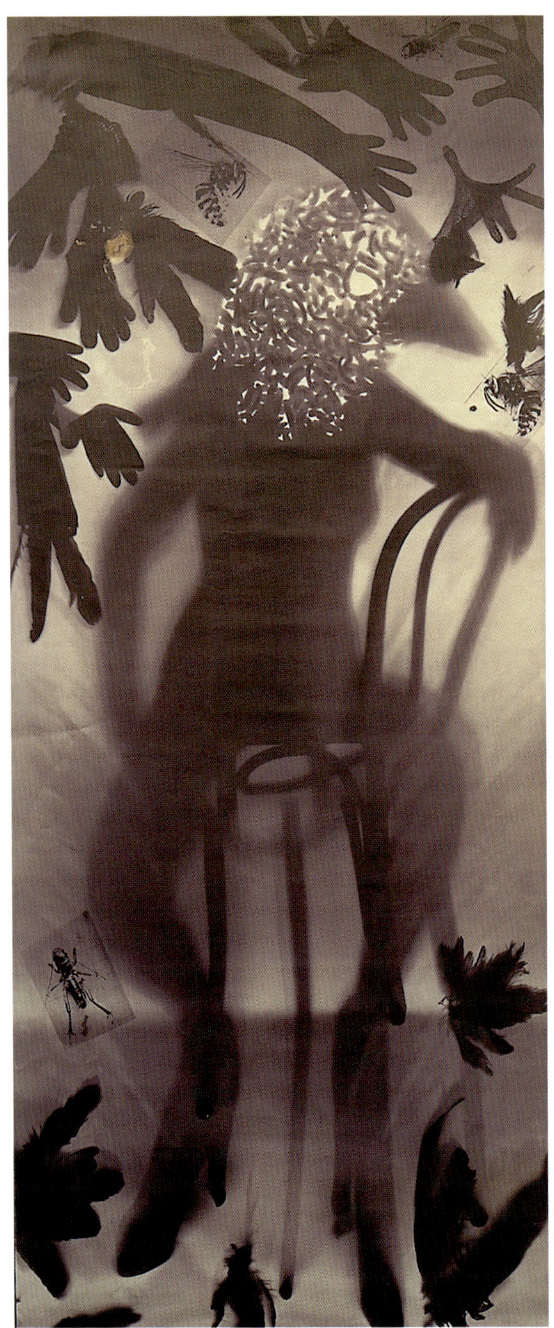

Virgil Mirano, *Bird Girl*, 1974, diazo cloth, 36½x86½ inches.

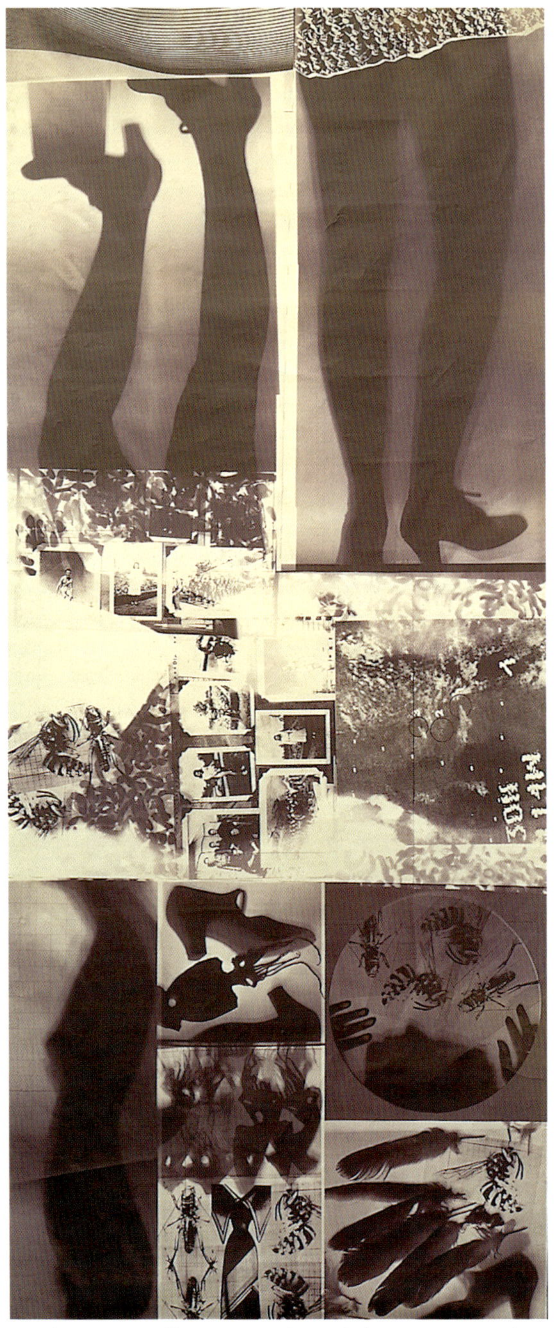

Virgil Mirano, *Walking*, 1973, diazo cloth, 36½x84¼ inches.

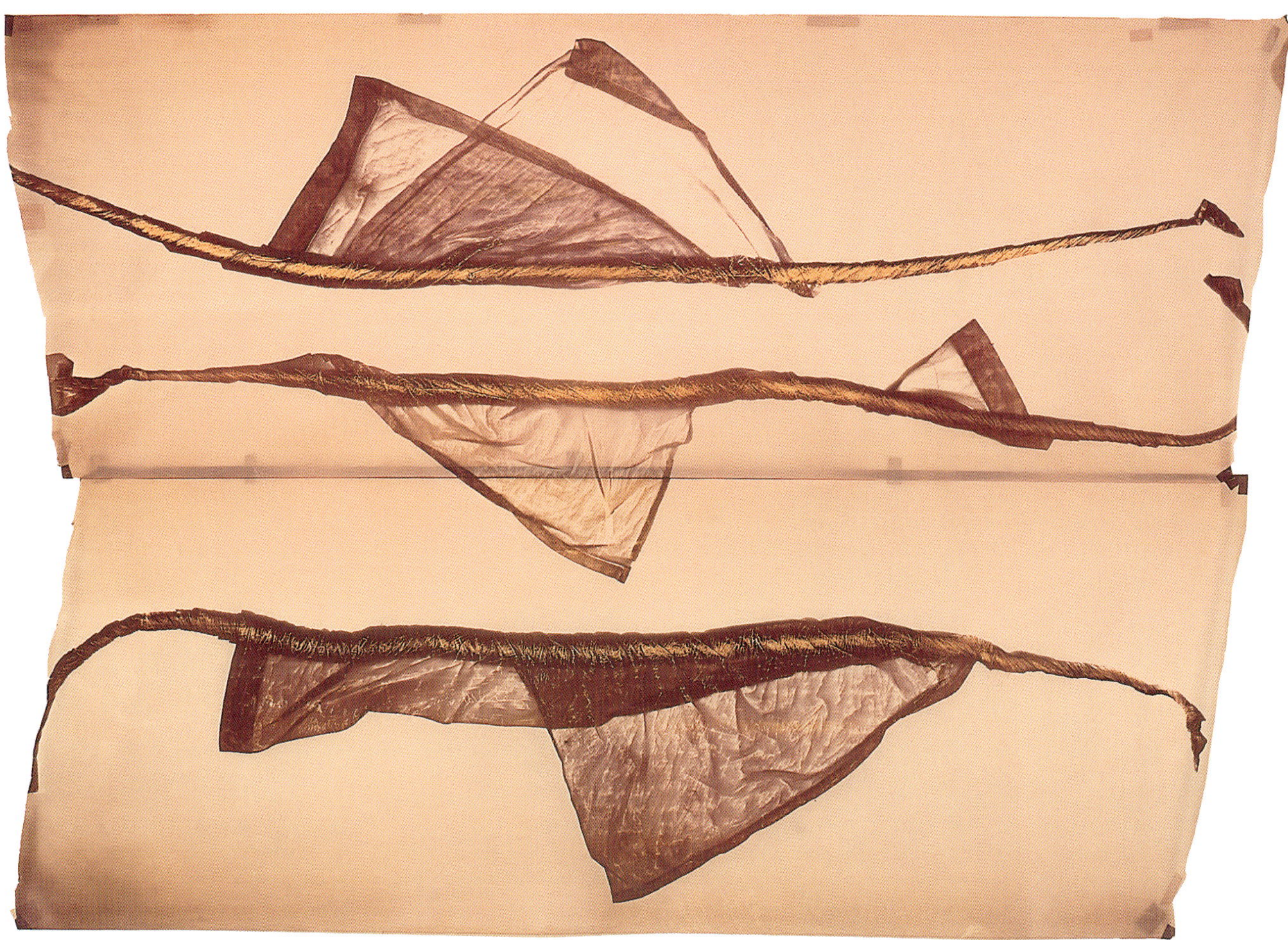

Virgil Mirano, *Flight*, 1976, diazo paper on canvas backing, 72x105 inches.

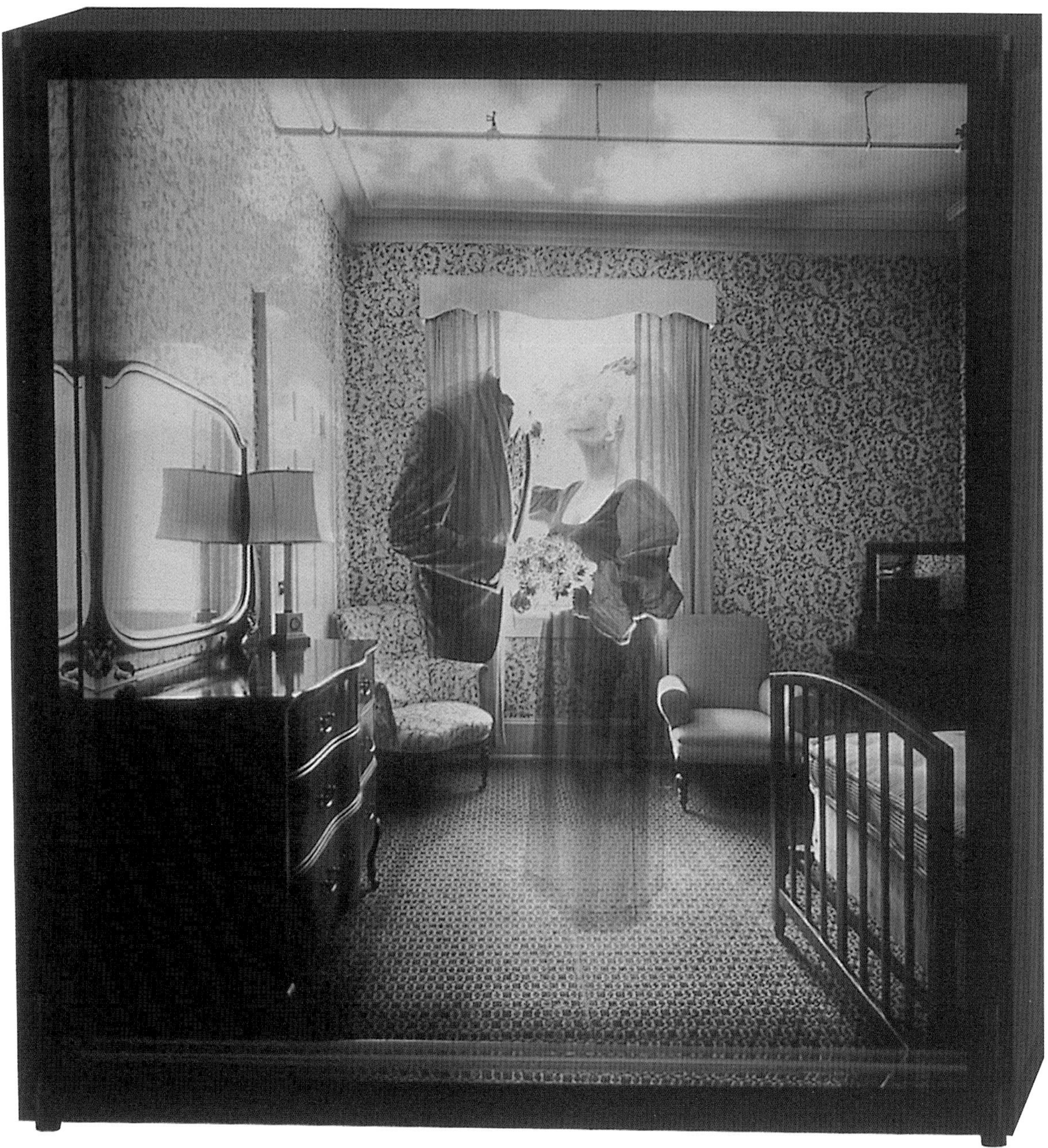

Doug Prince, *Wedding Chamber*, 1972, sculpture, 5x5x2½ inches.

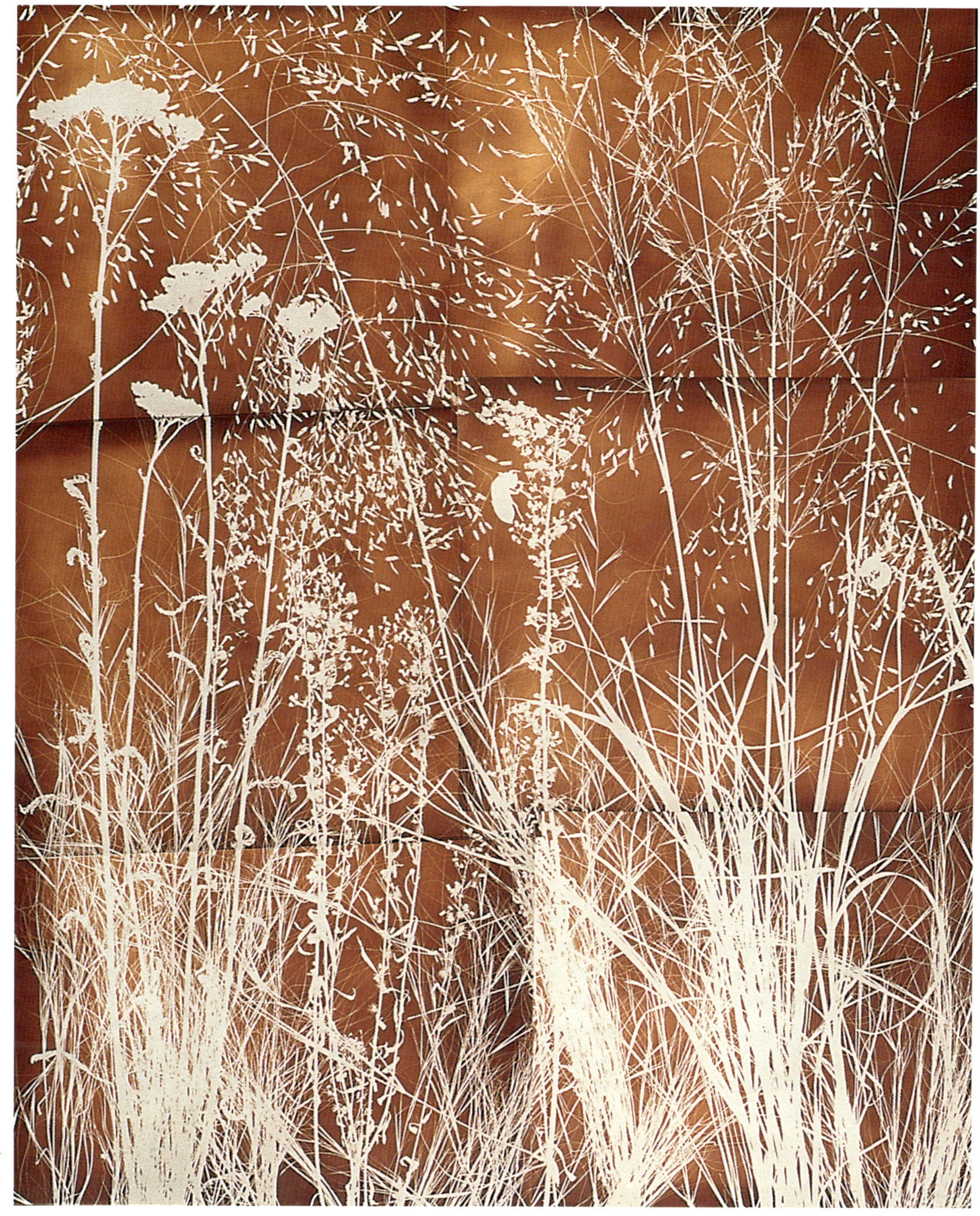

Doug Prince, *Plant print —Grasses*, 1994, photogram, 20x24 inches.

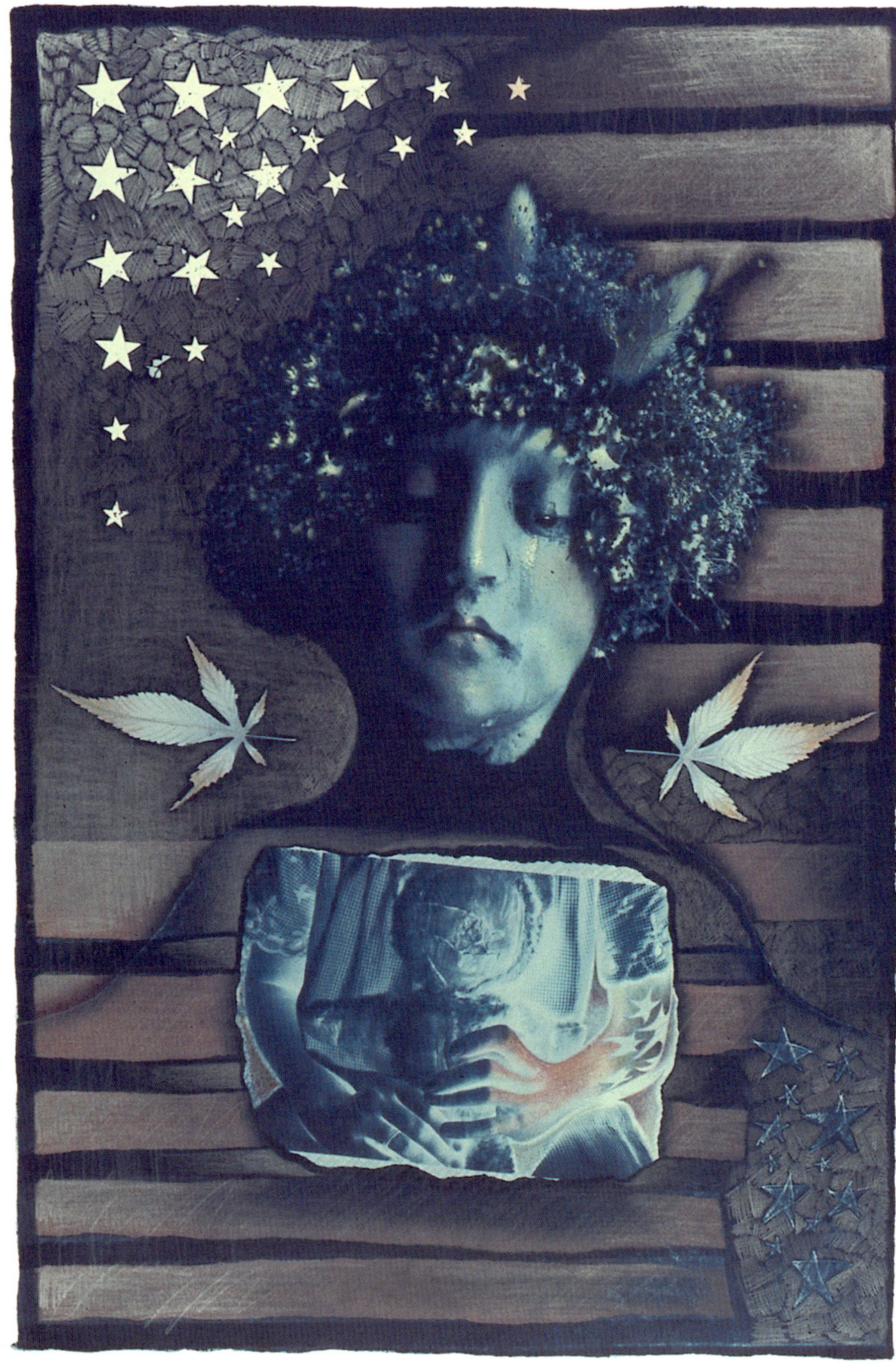

Evon Streetman, *American Gothic blueprint*, 1978, blueprint, hand coloring, 22x30 inches.

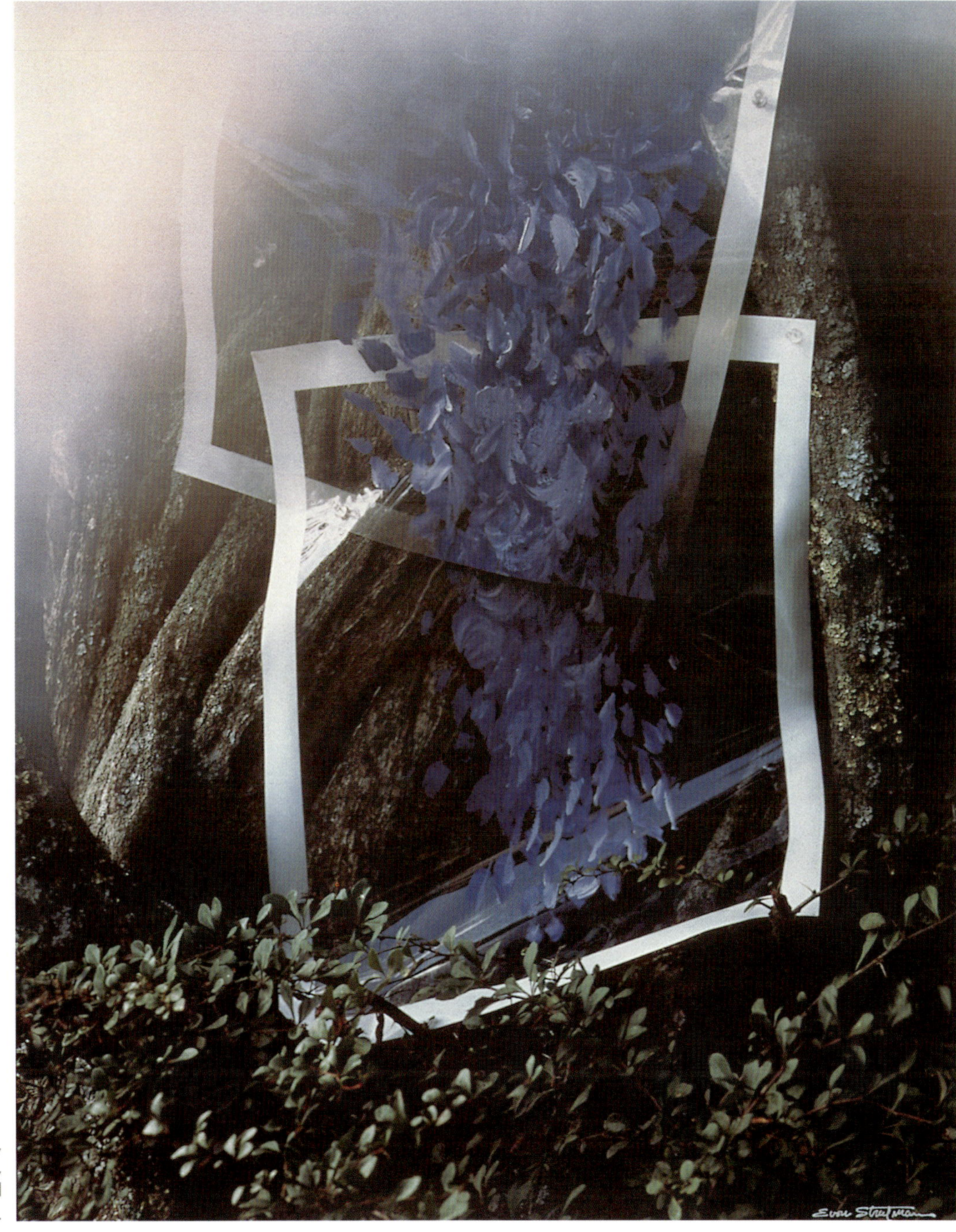


Evon Streetman, *Reflections & Wisteria*, 1983, cibachrome and acrylic, 24x31 inches.

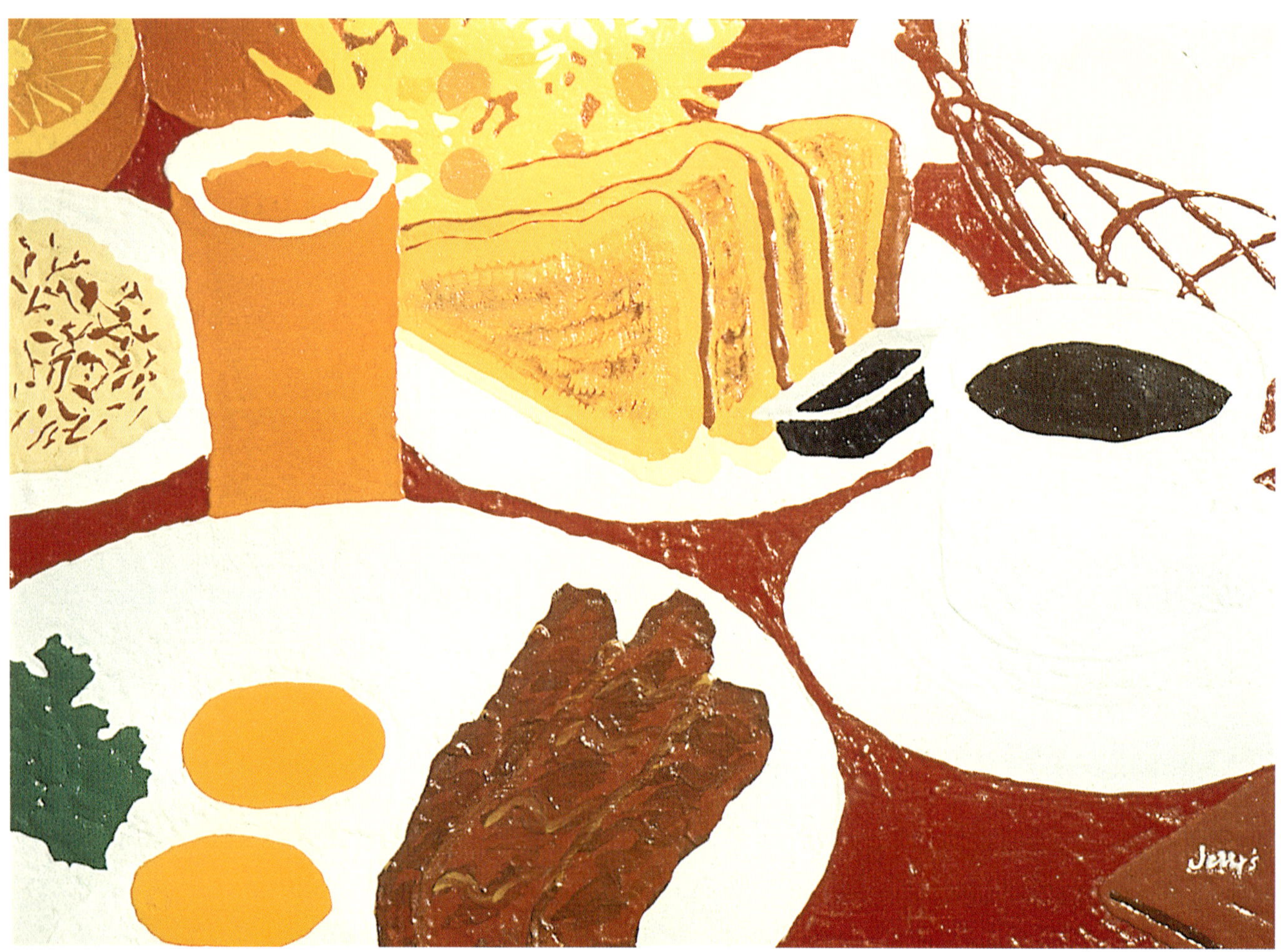

Tyler Turkle, *Mona Breakfast*, 1976, poured acrylic on velvet, 33x46 inches. Courtesy of Tricia Collins Contemporary Art, New York, New York.

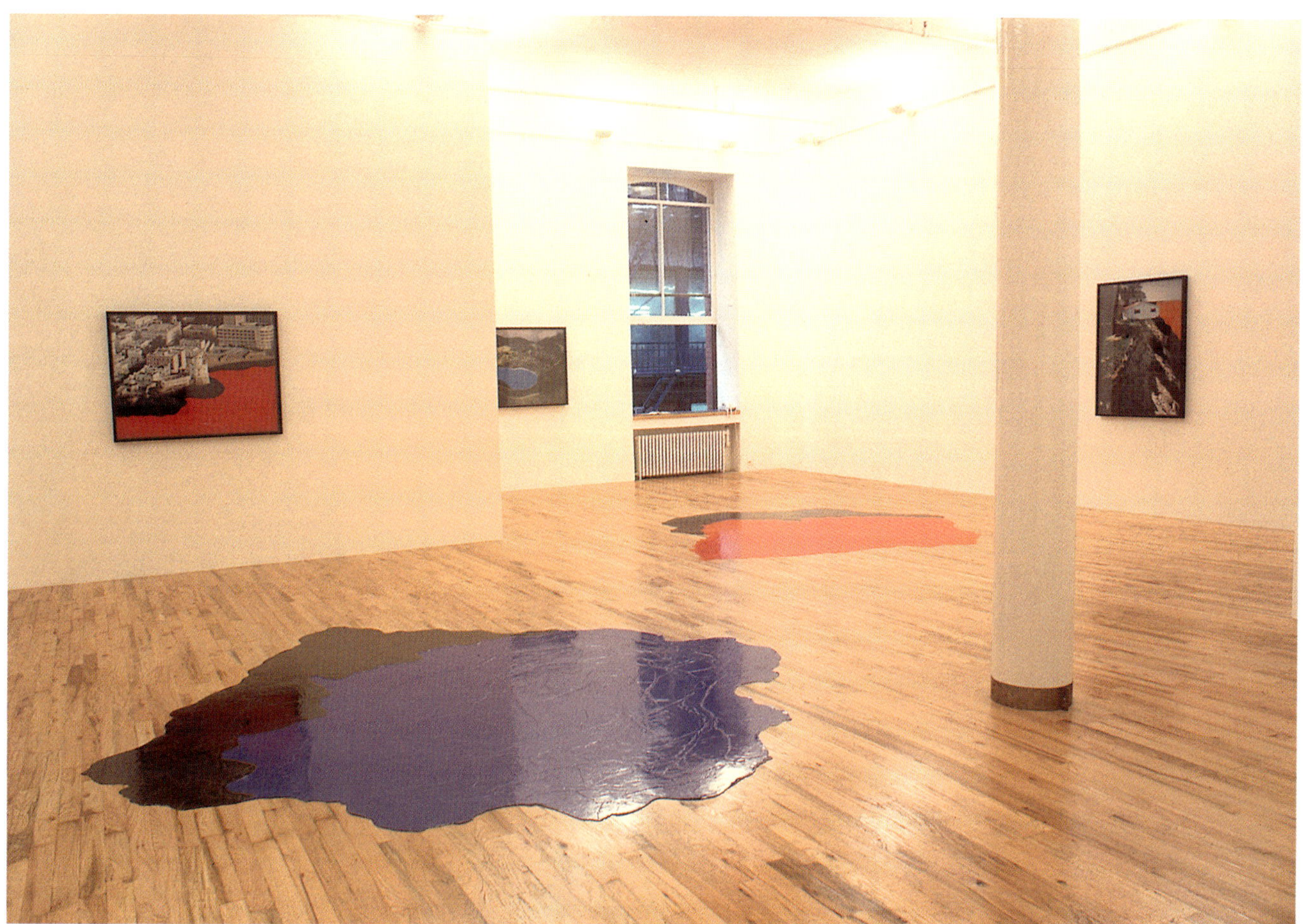

Tyler Turkle, *Plastic Water* and *Last Criterion* Installation at Greenberg Wilson Gallery, New York, New York, 1989.

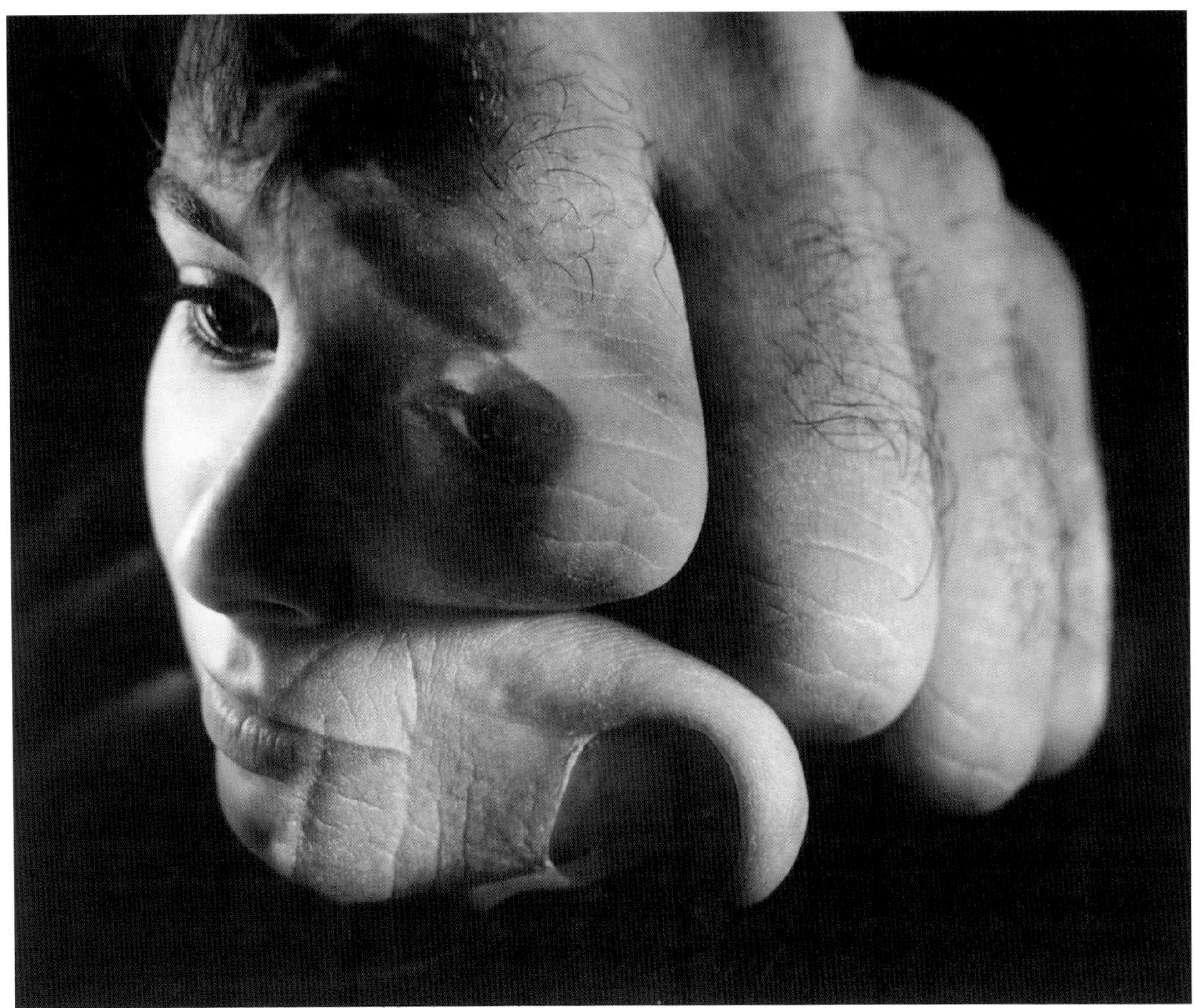

Jerry Uelsmann, *Symbolic Mutation*, 1961, silver gelatin print, 7x8 inches.

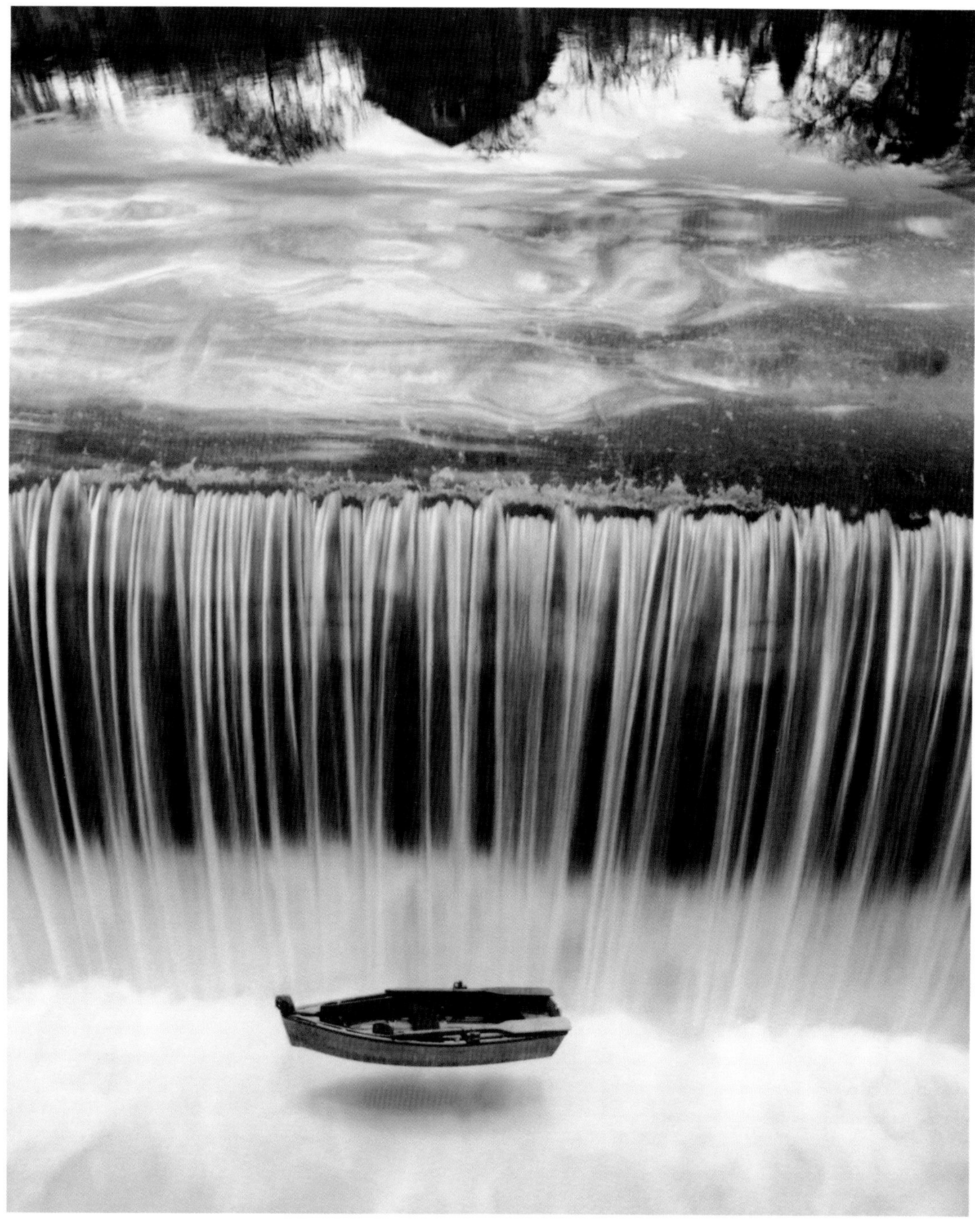

Jerry Uelsmann, *Untitled*, 1997, silver gelatin print, 16x20 inches.

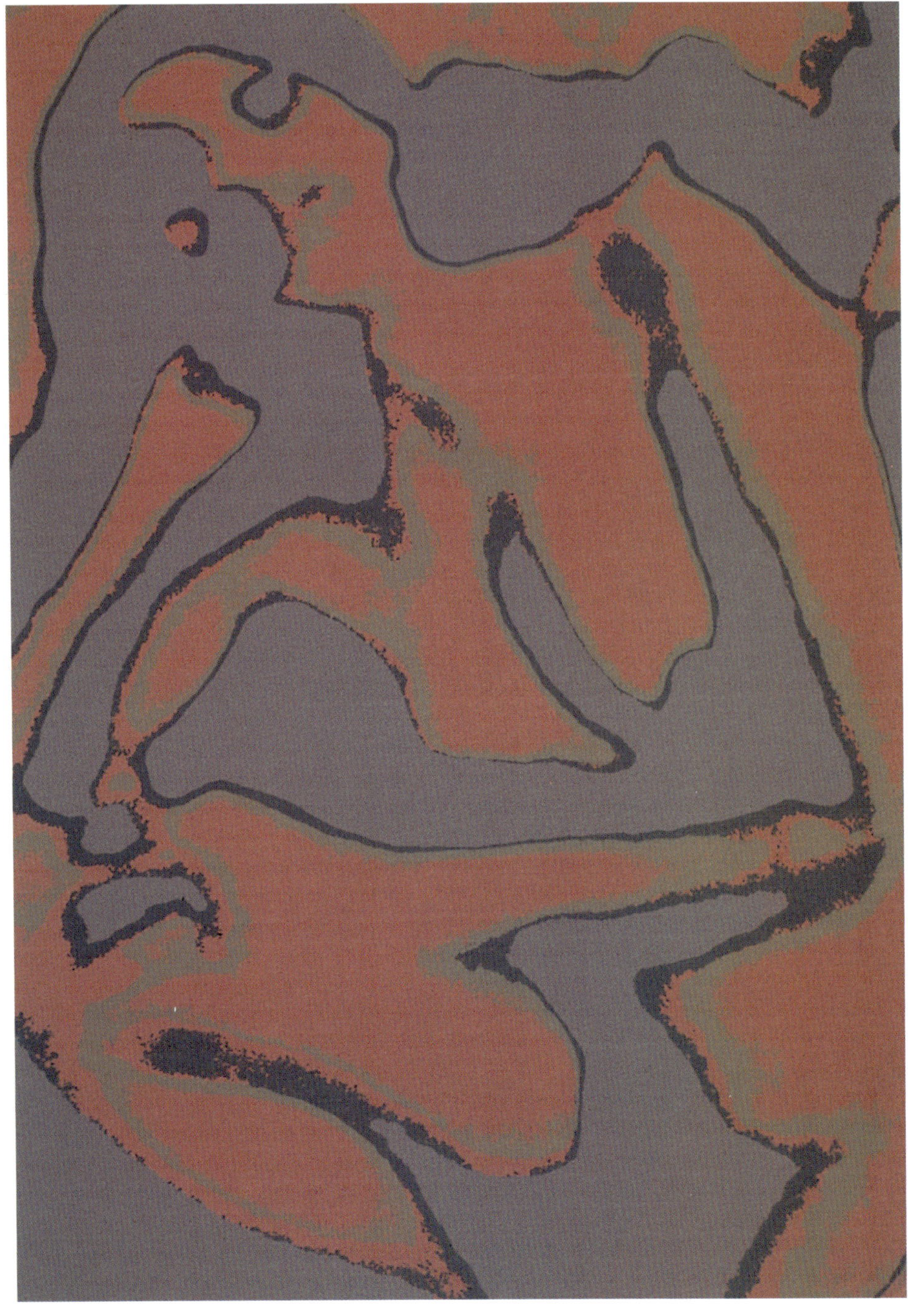

Todd Walker, *Sally, abstract orange,* 1972, silkscreen, 13x9¾ inches.

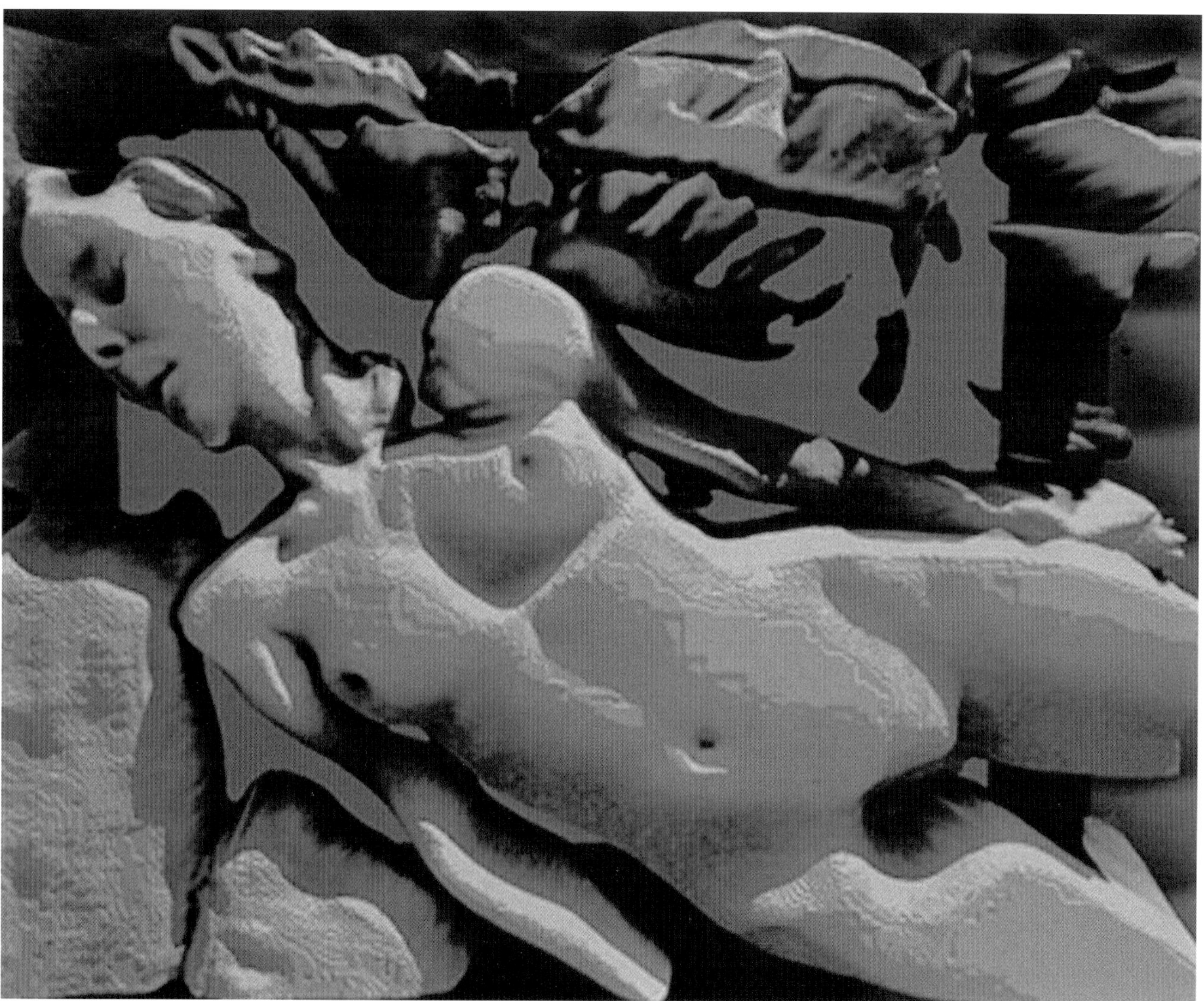

Todd Walker, *Deqpam*, 1990s, Epson archival print, 12¼x15½ inches.

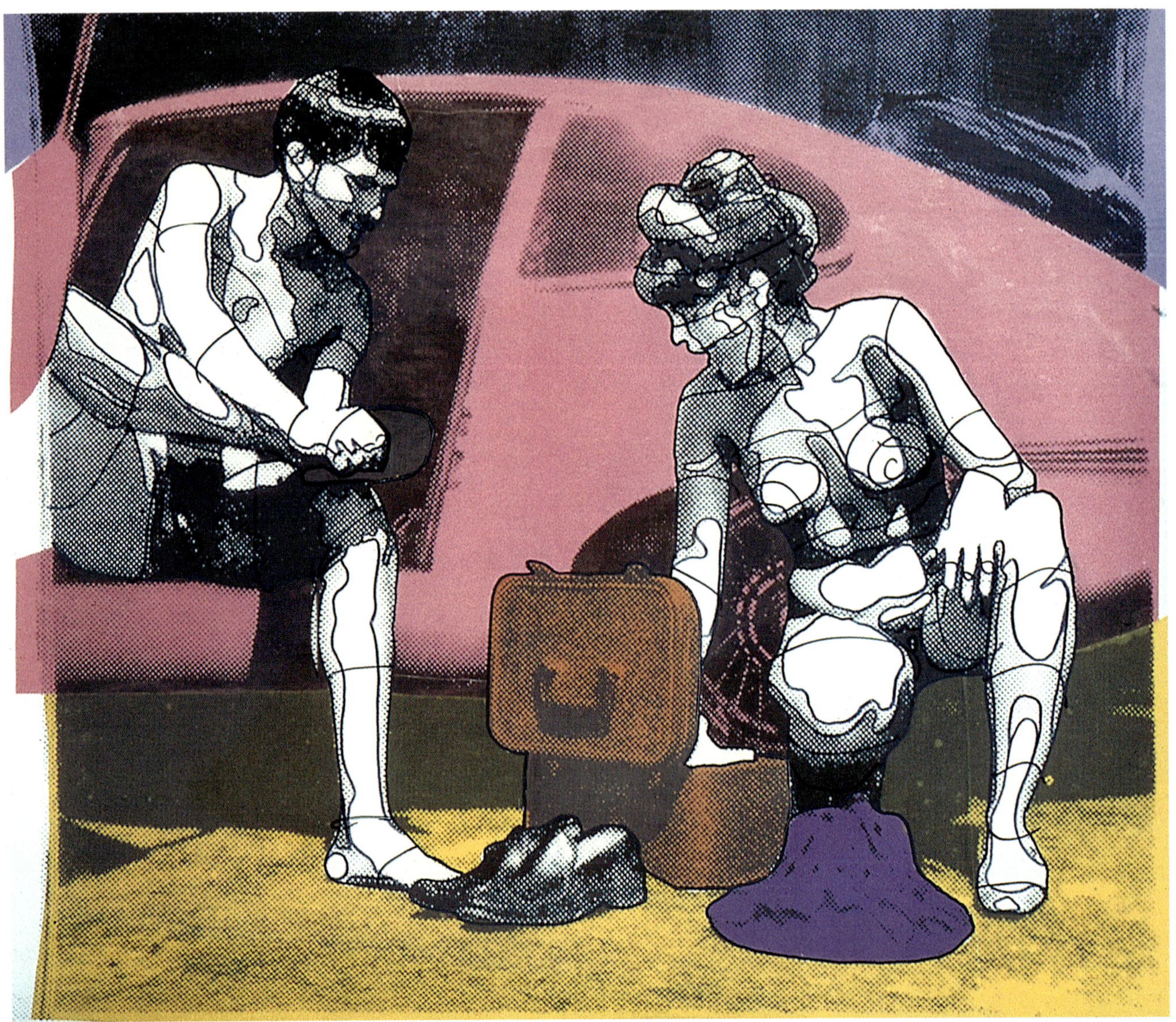

Wallace Wilson, *Nudist One*, 1979, color photograph, 20x24 inches.

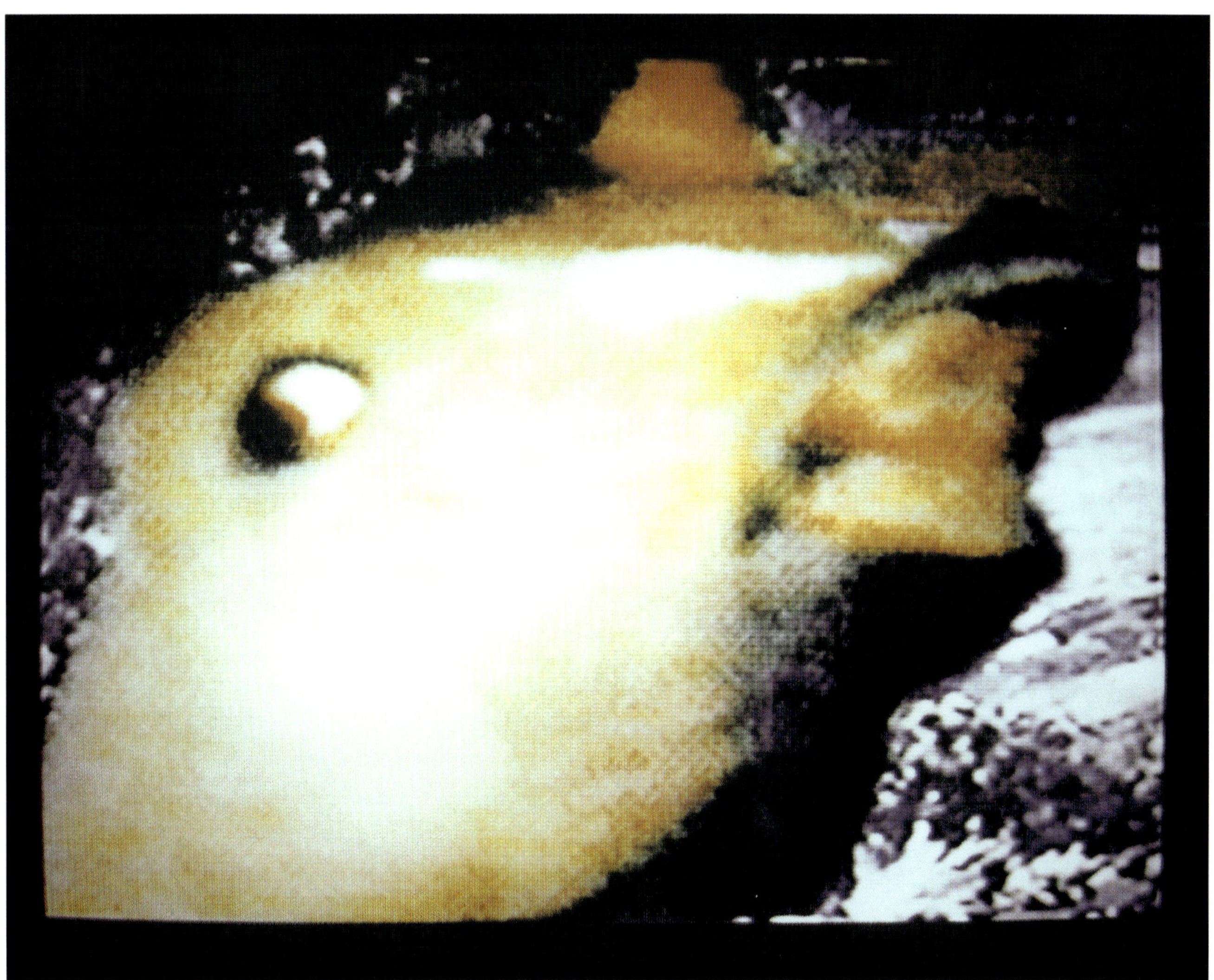

Wallace Wilson, *Distorted Transmission*, 1996, backlighted digital color acetate photograph, 40x50 inches.

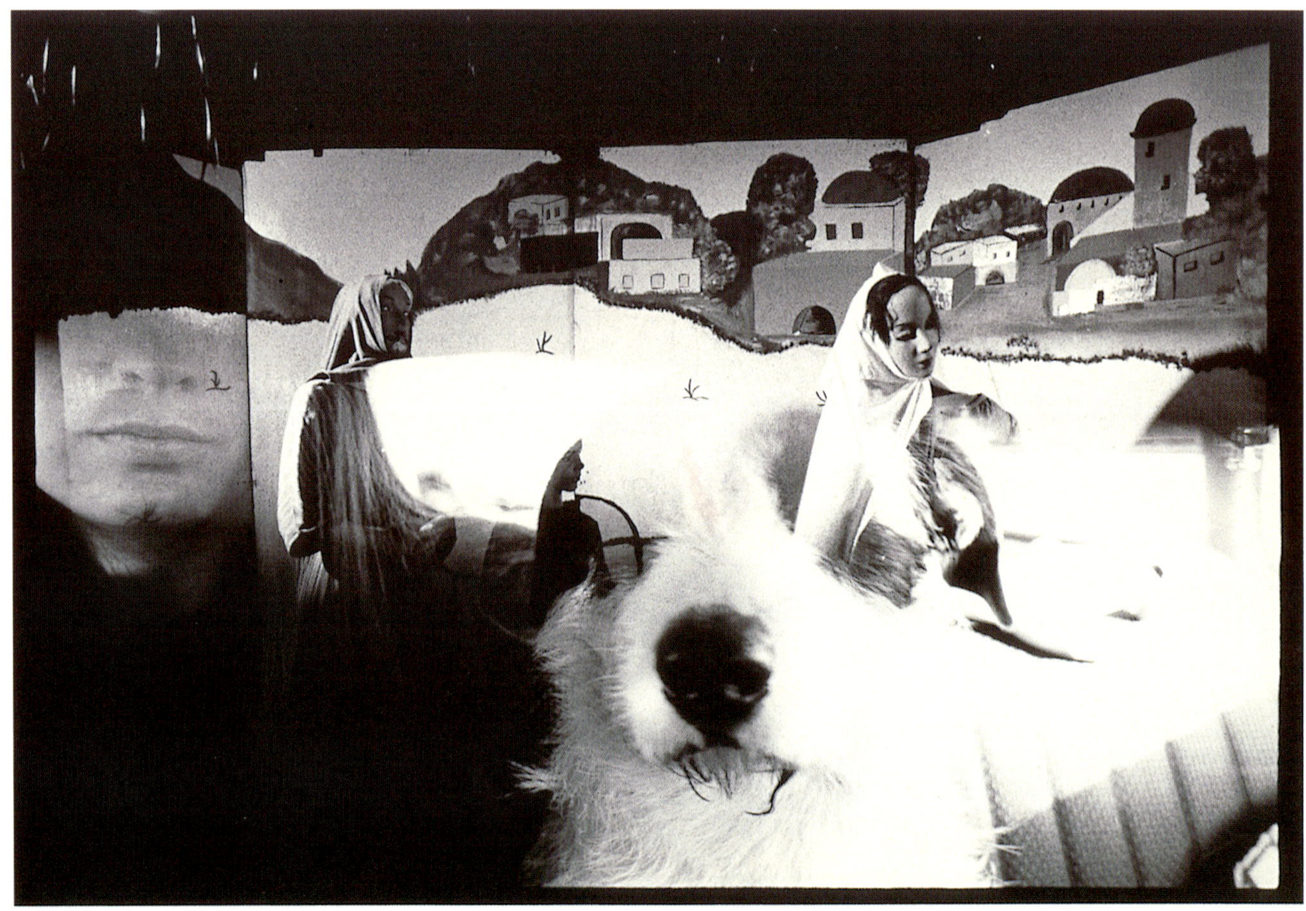

David Yager, from the series Hollywood, 1972-73, silver gelatin print, 11x14 inches.

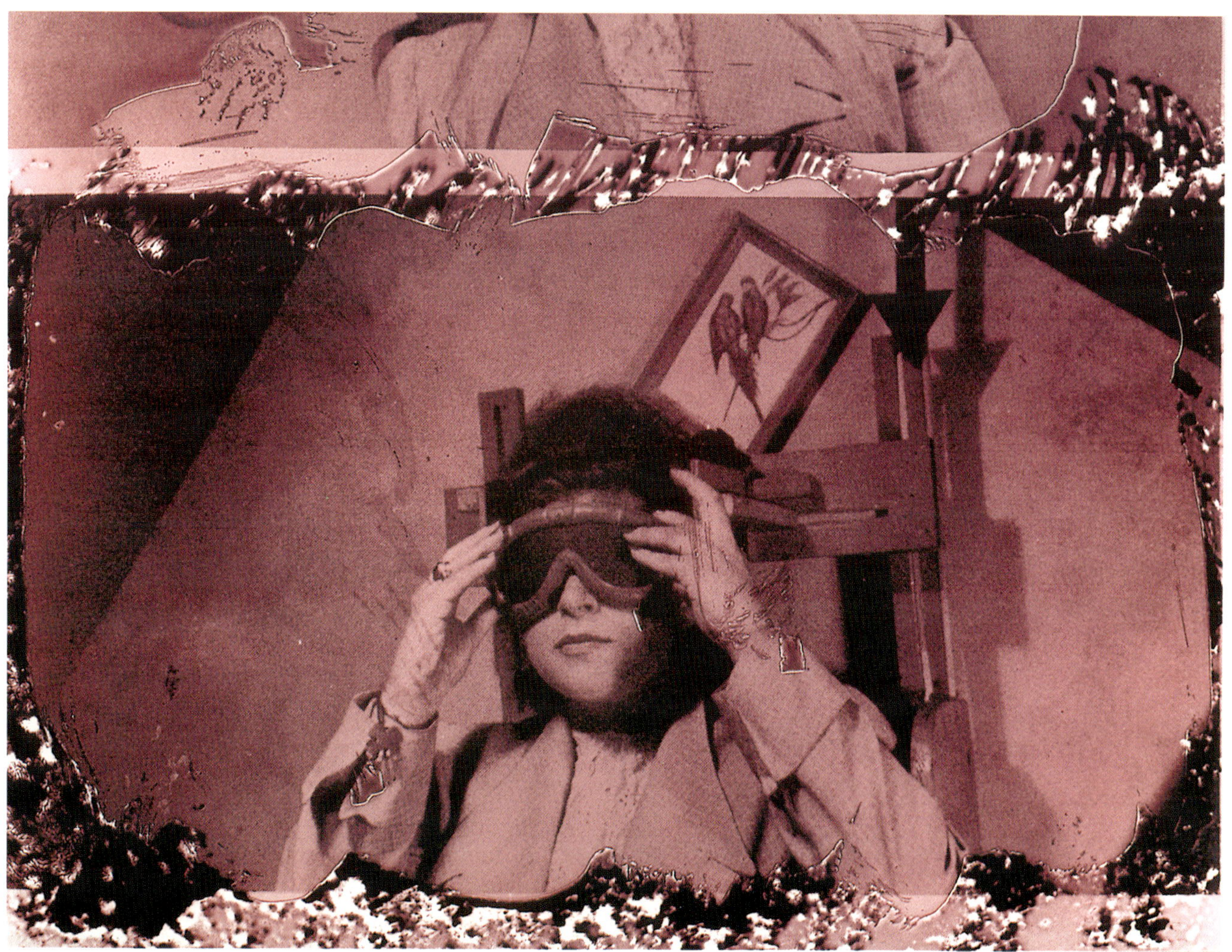

David Yager, from the series Education, Medicine, Science, 1999, Type C print, 29x28 inches.

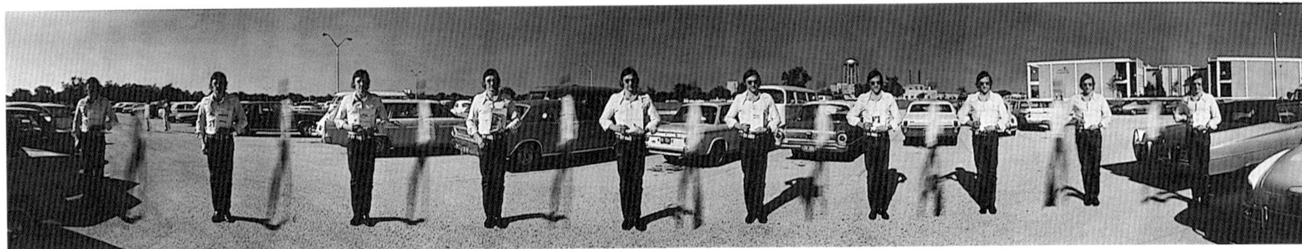

Oscar Bailey, *Ed Ruscha, 10 Times*, Tampa, FL, 1970, cirkut, 6x43 inches.

## OSCAR BAILEY

Oscar Bailey was born in Barnesville, Ohio, in 1925. He earned a BA in art from Wilmington College, Ohio, and began working as a commercial printer. In 1958, he graduated from Ohio University with his MFA in photography, subsequently began teaching at New York State University College in Buffalo, and in 1962 became a founding member of the Society of Photographic Education, a national organization for photography instructors. Bailey acquired his first Cirkut camera in the late 1960s. A Photography Professor at University of South Florida, Tampa, in 1969, he actively contributed to programs at Graphicstudio up to his retirement in 1985. Bailey has also taught photography at Penland School of Crafts in North Carolina; he has been Artist-in-Residence at ArtPark in Lewiston, New York (1977). In 1972, he assisted with the publication, *Silver Bullets*, a USF collection of student art work. Throughout his career, he has participated in numerous exhibitions, such as *The Sense of Abstraction in Contemporary Photography*, Museum of Modern Art, 1960; *Photography in the Twentieth Century*, National Gallery of Canada, 1967; and *Panoramic Photography*, The Photographic Galley, Southampton, England, 1981. He was awarded a Photographer's Fellowship from the National Endowment for the Arts in 1976. Since his retirement, he has moved to Burnsville, North Carolina, where he continues his interest in photography.

- *Statue, Ohio*, 1970, silver gelatin print, 10x13 inches.
- *Ed Ruscha, 10 Times*, Tampa, FL, 1970, cirkut, 6x43 inches.
- *The Room*, 1972, cut, paste, and re-photograph, 15½x10½ inches.
- *Me—Shadow Series*, 1974, silver gelatin print, 5¾x8½ inches.
- four 1974 works each entitled *Me*; each silver gelatin print, 5x7 inches.
- *Death Valley, Ubehebe Crater*, 1974, silver gelatin print, 13x16 inches.
- *Hold it, Alfred*, 1977, cut and paste, 7½x9 inches.
- *Let's All Play with Judy*, 1978, 30 3-inch square wood blocks, 16½x19¾ inches.
- *Snapshot Cirkut, Carolina Hemlock, NC*, 1979, cirkut photo plus cut and photogram, 7½x47 inches.
- *Statues, Florida*, 1980, silver gelatin print, 10½x12½ inches.
- *Expressway Interchange, Miami, FL*, 1980, cirkut, 10x60½ inches.
- *Feed Lot, Bartow, FL*, 1983, cirkut, 8x57 inches.
- *Oscar and Sara at Roan Mountain, NC*, 1983, cirkut, 10x57 inches.
- *Ochlocknee St. Park, FL*, 1983, cirkut, 10x56 inches.
- *Self Portrait*, 1984, blueprint, 8½x11 inches.
- *Oscar and Sara at Ouray, CO*, 1984, cirkut, 10x62 inches.
- *Oscar and Sara at Gateway Arch, St. Louis, MO*, 1984, cirkut, 10x63¼ inches.
- *Oscar and Sara at the Ormond Beach Hotel, FL*, 1987, cirkut, 8x59 inches.
- *Oscar and Sara at Chimayo, NM*, 1988, cirkut, 10x61 inches.

## GEORGE BLAKELY

Born 1951 in Long Beach, California, George Blakely attended California State University at Fullerton, where he received his BA in Business Administration and an MA in Design. In 1978, he earned his MFA in Photography from Tyler School of Art, Philadelphia, Pennsylvania. The same year he took a position in Florida State University's Art Department. Along with his teaching position, Blakely serves as a Visiting Lecturer at institutions throughout the nation. He received two National Endowment of the Arts Photography Fellowships (1979, 1988), Fine Arts Council of Florida Individual Artist Fellowships (1979, 1986, and 1996), and the James D. Phelan Award in Sculpture

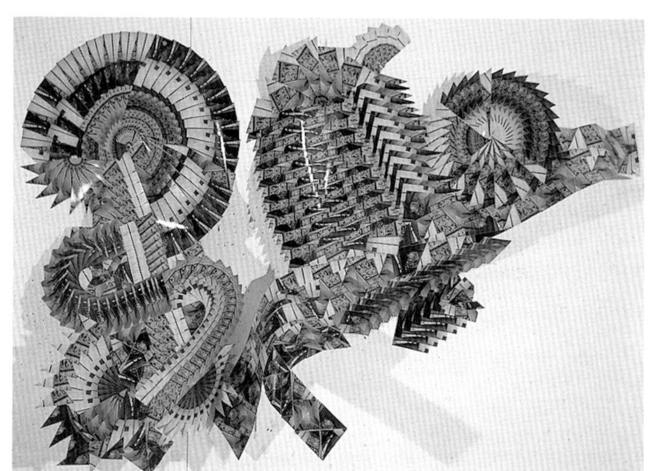

George Blakely, detail of *Florida Postcards* installation, 1981, 48x36 inches.

(1978). Since the 1970s, Blakely has exhibited his works in over twenty-five solo shows and two hundred group shows. He is also recognized as Guest Curator for *BANG! The Gun as Image: The Gun Depicted in Our Culture* and *Photo Invitational II*, both at the Florida State University Museum of Fine Arts, as well as many student shows throughout the area. Blakely continues to serve on the faculty at Florida State University.

- *A Cubic Foot of Photographs*, 1978, wire-bound photographs, c. one foot square each side (one cubic foot).
- *Snapshot Delineation*, c. 1978, 20x25 inches.
- *Florida Postcards,* installation excerpt, 1981, 48x36 inches.
- *Beaumont Newhall's History*, 1987, 6x8 feet.
- *Junk Mail Poles* (3), 1988-ongoing, dimensions variable.
- *Lemons, Marlborough Man, Mohammed Ali*, 1990, 21x25 inches each.
- *Tablets* (9), 1993-1996, installation dimensions variable.
- *Face Poles* (9), 1996, installation dimensions variable: three poles 2 inches x 11 feet; three poles one inch x 8 feet; three poles 1½ inches by 9 feet.
- *We Clowns* (9), 1999, ink jet prints, mounted flush in grid, 30x30 inches each.
- two *Sink / Floats*, 2000; one sink / float 13x4x5 inches; one sink / float 14x3½x3½ inches.

## VAN DEREN COKE

Van Deren Coke was born July 4, 1921, in Lexington, Kentucky. He received an AB in history and art history from the University of Kentucky, Lexington, and an MFA in art history and sculpture from Indiana University, Bloomington, also attending summer classes at Harvard University and studying at Clarence White School of Photography. He also studied with Nicholas Haz and Ansel Adams. His academic posts include: University of Florida, Gainesville; Arizona State University, Tempe; St. Martin's School of Art, London; and Elam School of Fine Arts, University of Auckland, New Zealand. Coke also served as Chair of the Art Department and Director of the Art Museum of the University of New Mexico, of the International Museum of Photography at George Eastman House, and as Head of the Department of Photography, San Francisco Museum of Modern Art. His long list of honors and awards include: Photography International Award, 1955-1957; Guggenheim Fellowship, 1975; Honorary Doctorate of Humane Letters from the Academy of Art, San Francisco, 1986; Leica Medal of Excellence "Educator of the Year," granted by E. Leitz Corp., 1988; Senior Fulbright Fellowship, New Zealand, 1989; and Distinguished International Career in Photography Award, 1992. Along with his studio and teaching careers, the Artist has had a distinguished curatorial career [please see *Interview* preceding] and has recently curated: *Twenty-one Photographers from New*

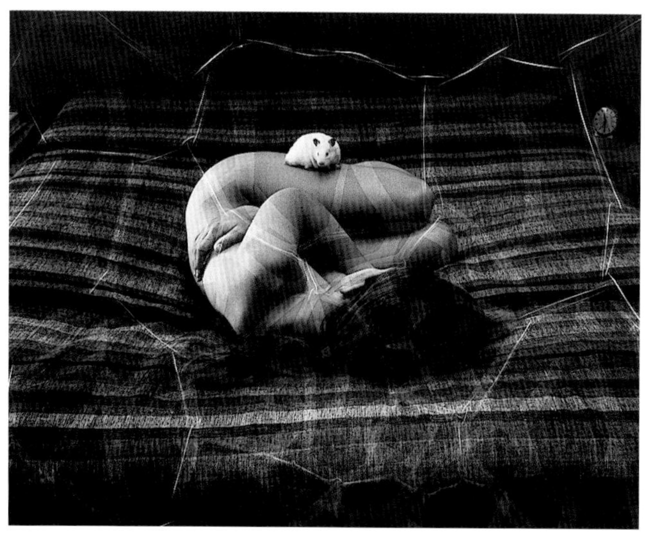

Van Deren Coke, *Homage to Munch No. 2*, 1960, silver gelatin print, 10½x13⅛ inches.

Mexico, Vision Gallery, San Francisco, 1991; *Three Generations of Hispanic Photographers Working in New Mexico*, The Harwood Foundation Museum of the University of New Mexico, Taos, 1993; and *Forecast: Shifts in Direction*, Museum of Fine Arts, Santa Fe, New Mexico, 1994. His photographs have been shown in countless solo and group exhibitions in the States and abroad, and his seminal book *The Painter and the Photograph* (1964, UNM Press), set the bar for all subsequent discussions on the topic.

- *Homage to Munch No. 1*, 1955, silver gelatin print, 10½x 13½ inches.
- *Death of a Flower*, 1956, silver gelatin print, 11x10½ inches.
- *Dying Sea Gull*, 1958, silver gelatin print, 10⅓x11¾ inches.
- *Dead Bird in Flight*, 1958, silver gelatin print, 10⅓x13½ inches.
- *Tar Mired Turtle and Dead Fish*, 1958, silver gelatin print, 10½x13½ inches.
- *Grand Ma in Florida*, 1960, silver gelatin print, 12⅝x10½ inches.
- *Remains of Sun Dried Fish*, 1960, silver gelatin print, 10½x 13½ inches.
- *Homage to Munch No. 2*, 1960, silver gelatin print, 10½x 13⅛ inches.
- *Dessicated Rodent*, 1961, silver gelatin print, 9¼x10¾ inches.
- *Christ in Florida*, 1961, silver gelatin print, 13½x10½ inches.
- *A Memorial Bust of Lorca the Poet, Mexico City*, 1984, cibachrome print, 8½x13¾ inches.
- *Head of an 18th Century Virgin, Patzcuaro, Mexico*, 1984, cibachrome print, 9¾x13¾ inches.
- *Ceramic Face on a Planter, Tzintzuntzan, Mexico*, 1988, cibachrome print, 7⅞x8⅞ inches.
- *Caja, Mexico City*, 1988, cibachrome print, 6⅝x9⅞ inches.
- *Mexico Piece by Aguilar, Ocatlán, Mexico*, 1991, cibachrome print, 9⅓x7⅓ inches.
- *A White Mouse Cursing (Bird Dropping Art)*, from *Looking Down* Series, 1995, Type C print, 6⅞x10½ inches.
- *A Black Musician and Snake*, from *Looking Down* Series, 1997, Type C print, 9x7⅝ inches.
- *Muscle Man*, from *Looking Down* Series, 1999, Type C print, 11⅝x9⅓ inches.
- *Wounded Warrior*, from *Looking Down* Series, 1999, Type C print, 13½x9⅓ inches.
- *Man with a Big Shadow*, from *Looking Down* Series, 1999, Type C print, 9¼x11 inches.

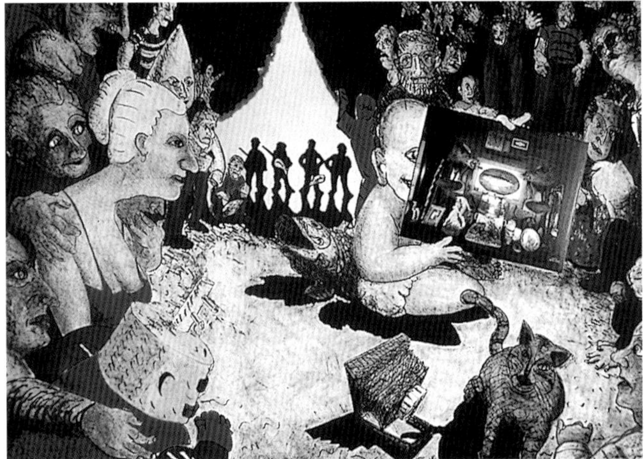

Robert W. Fichter, *Time Is, Baby Gene Pool's First Photo*, 1979, lithograph with albumen print insert.

## ROBERT W. FICHTER

Robert W. Fichter was born in Ft. Myers, Florida, in 1939. He received his BFA in painting and printmaking from the University of Florida where he studied photography with Jerry Uelsmann. He went to Indiana University to study with Henry Holmes Smith and got an MFA in photography and printmaking in 1966. He joined the staff at the George Eastman House as a junior curator to work with Nathan Lyons. His first full time teaching position was at UCLA. In 1972 he joined the faculty at Florida State University where he is currently a Professor of Art. He has also taught at the Art Institute of Chicago, the University of Florida and the Penland School of Crafts. He has lectured, given workshops and exhibited his work extensively. The exhibition *Robert Fichter, Photography and Other Questions* was developed and curated by Robert A. Sobieszek for the International Museum of Photography at George Eastman House, Rochester, New York; the catalogue of exhibition was published in 1983 by the University of New Mexico Press, the International Museum of Photography at George Eastman House and Robert Friedus Gallery, New York, New York. His work is in the collections of many museums and institutions including: the George Eastman House Museum, Rochester, New York; the National Gallery in Washington, DC; the Los Angeles County Museum; and the Canadian National Gallery. Previous exhibitions organized for Florida State University

Museum of Fine Arts include: *Photophantasists* (1973), a survey of American contemporary photography; *Colors* (1975), an exhibition of photo/artists working in various printmaking media; and *Photo Language Notes* in the early '80s. An offset portfolio of original art works, by the artists, documented the exhibition *Colors* and was produced with support from the National Endowment for the Arts. Robert Fichter has also received Individual Artist Fellowships from the Florida Arts Council and from the National Endowment for the Arts.

- *Roast Beast Weapon of War, 1970*, 1970, blueprint, gum print, 12x18 inches.
- *Photo Info #2*, 1972, Inko dye, 23x19 inches.
- *Okra*, 1975, blueprint, air brush, 25½x35 inches.
- *Peace in the Kingdom*, 1975, blueprint, air brush, 25x39 inches.
- *Time Is, Baby Gene Pool's First Photo*, 1979, lithograph with albumen print insert.
- *Bones to Baby Gene Pool: "It's Just Like Life Flashing before Your Eyes,"* 1979, lithograph with color separation.
- *Bones Alone Has Looked on Beauty Bare*, 1980, lithograph (Tamarind), photolitho insert, 45x 31¼ inches.
- *Ma Bell Madonna*, 1981, cibachrome, 31x25 inches.
- *Waiting for the Signal*, 1981, cibachrome, 37x29½ inches.
- *Hiroshima Memorial #1*, 1981, cibachrome, 36x24½ inches.
- *Durer with Red Flowers*, 1984, cibachrome print, 29x23 inches.
- *Distress Signal*, 1984, cibachrome, 36x29½ inches.
- *Hand of Man*, 1984, cibachrome, 35x28½ inches.
- *Aid to Memory*, nd, painting with Type C photo insert, 77½x65½ inches.
- *Atom Struck Tile, the Explosion Center Hiroshima, Shado/ Light*, 1984, aquatint with photo offset insert, 26½x34 inches.
- *Southern View #1: Forest Management*, 1999, Type C print, 20x24 inches.

## VIRGIL MIRANO

Born January 3, 1937, in Los Angeles, California, Virgil Mirano obtained a BA from California State University and an MFA from UCLA. He has led an active career as a photographer both in the studio and in the film industry. In 1965, he began his career working for the Design Office of Charles and Ray Eames. Later, he worked as an instructor of photography at various universities, including UCLA, Florida State University, and the Art Institute of Chicago. In the late 1970s, Mirano continued his interest in motion pictures by assisting on the film *Gal Young 'Un* as a Lighting Advisor; he served as Special Visual Consultant for *Star Trek The Movie*. He has been the Director of Still Photography for Robert Abels & Associates, Entertainment Effects Groups, and Boss Films Studios. Throughout his career, Mirano has worked on still/visuals for feature films, like *Ghostbusters*, *Independence Day* and *Titanic*. He has also worked on a number of independent pictures through Nunez films; for *Ruby in Paradise* he served as Lighting Consultant and was Director of Photography for *Ulee's Gold*. Currently, he lives in California, making films and taking photographs.

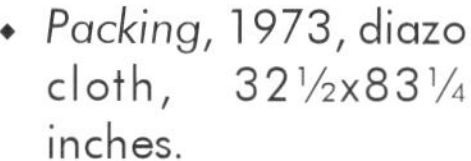

- *Packing*, 1973, diazo cloth, 32½x83¼ inches.
- *Walking*, 1973, diazo cloth, 36½x84¼ inches.
- *Knots*, 1973, diazo paper on canvas backing, 72x105 inches.
- *He/She 1*, 1973, diazo paper with canvas backing, 77¾x36 inches.
- *He/She 2*, 1973, diazo paper with canvas backing, 77¾x36 inches.
- *No Witness*, 1973, diazo paper with canvas backing, 82x36 inches.
- *Gravity*, 1974, diazo paper with canvas backing, 36x97

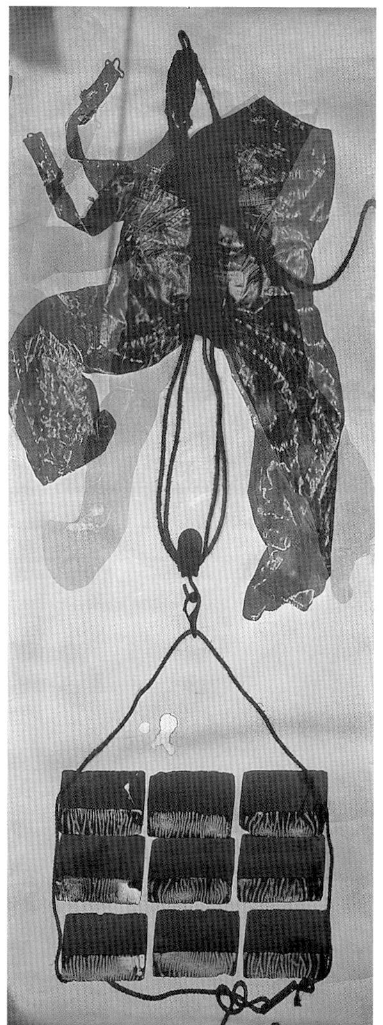

Virgil Mirano, *Gravity*, 1974, diazo paper with canvas backing, 36x97 inches.

inches.

- *Bird Girl*, 1974, diazo cloth, 36½x86½ inches.
- *Flight*, 1976, diazo paper on canvas backing, 72x105 inches.
- *Robert's Gift*, 1999, VHS, 13 minutes15 seconds.
- *Scientific and Industrial Props*, 2000, VHS, 8 minutes.

## DOUG PRINCE

Doug Prince was born in 1943. He earned both his BA in Fine Arts and MA in Photography from the University of Iowa. Since the late 1960s, he has held teaching positions at various universities including the University of Florida, Rhode Island School of Design, and Syracuse University. Prince has been the recipient of two National Endowment of the Arts Fellowships and a New York Foundation of the Arts Artist's Fellowship. Since the mid-1960s, he has exhibited at various museums and galleries within the United States and abroad. A few of his most recent exhibitions include *The Body*, a summer festival in Skopelos, Greece; *Desire*, Musée de l'Eysée, Lausanne, Switzerland; *Photography's Multiple Roles*, The Museum of Contemporary Photography, Chicago; and *Moments in Time: Master Photographs from the Currier*, The Currier Gallery of Art, Manchester, New Hampshire; *Light Construction*, Johnson Museum, Cornell University. This year, Northern Kentucky University mounted a one-person exhibition and published a catalogue titled: *All Possible Worlds*. This exhibition subsequently traveled to the Houston Center of Photography. Prince has lived in Portsmouth, New Hampshire, since 1991 and works as a photographer at the University of New Hampshire/ Durham.

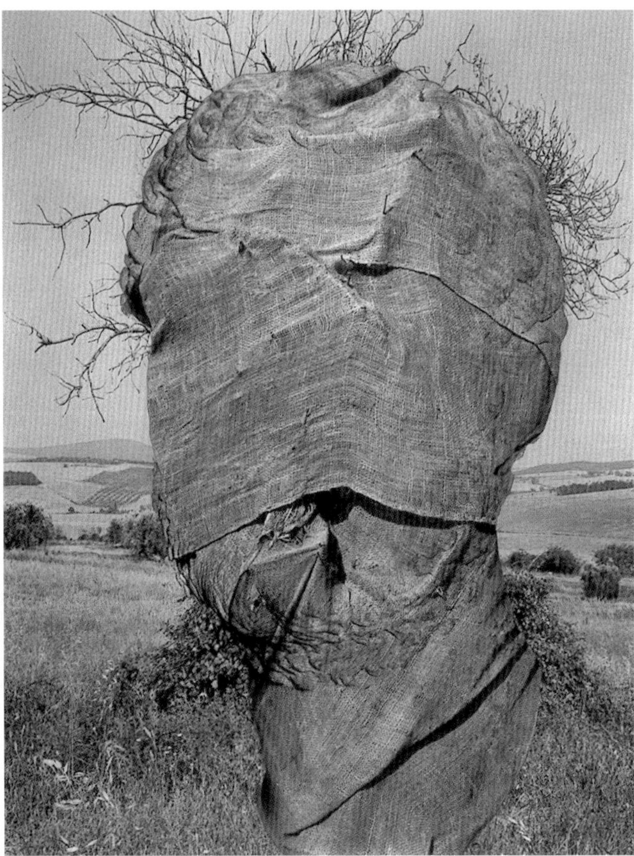

Doug Prince, *Transfiguration #34*, 1990, silver gelatin print, 11x14 inches.

- *Winter Funeral*, 1970, film and plastic, 5x5x2½ inches.
- *Magnolia Chamber*, 1972, film and plastic, 5x5x2½ inches.
- *Wedding Chamber*, 1972, film and plastic, 5x5x2½ inches.
- *Alimentary Canal*, 1974, film and plastic, 5x5x2½ inches.
- *Brian and Circus Tent*, 1974, silver gelatin print, 11x14 inches.
- *Fireplace and Sand*, 1976, silver gelatin print, 11x14 inches.
- *Broken Bread*, 1978, film and plastic, 5x5x2½ inches.
- *Suspenders and Bed*, 1983, film and plastic, 5x5x 2½ inches.
- *Transfiguration #5*, 1988, silver gelatin print, 11x14 inches.
- *Transfiguration #34*, 1990, silver gelatin print, 11x14 inches.
- *Butterfly Print #1*, 1993, silver gelatin print, 11x14 inches.
- *Plant print—Rose*, 1994, photogram, 20x24 inches.
- *Plant print—Unknown*, 1994, photogram, 20x24 inches.
- *Plant print—Sunflower*, 1994, photogram, 20x24 inches.
- *Plant print—Grasses*, 1994, photogram, 20x24 inches.
- *Body Prints #12*, 1996, resist-silverprint, 20x24 inches.
- *Body Prints #8*, 1996, resist-silverprint, 20x24 inches.
- *Body Prints #9*, 1996, resist-silverprint, 20x24 inches.
- *Body Prints #6*, 1996, resist-silverprint, 20x24 inches.
- *Purgatory*, 1997, silver gelatin print, 11x14 inches.
- *Dog, Observatory and Moon*, 1999, digital print, 11x14 inches.
- *Body Image #1*, 1999, inkjet print, 11x14 inches.
- *Body Image #3*, 1999, inkjet print, 11x14 inches.
- *Body Image #8*, 1999, inkjet print, 11x14 inches.
- *Body Image #9*, 1999, inkjet print, 11x14 inches.
- *Brian with Running Statues*, 2000, silver gelatin print, 11x14 inches.

- *Topology #66*, 2000, inkjet print, 16x20 inches.
- *Topology #78*, 2000, inkjet print, 16x20 inches.

## EVON STREETMAN

On June 8, 1932, Evon Streetman was born in Ft. Meade, Florida. She attended Florida State University, where she obtained a BA in painting and began graduate studies in advertising design and painting. In 1956, she moved to New York City to explore her interest in photography and to freelance. Upon returning to Florida, Streetman opened her own commercial photographic studio, and later became an Assistant Professor at her alma mater, Florida State University. During the years from 1964 until 1975, Streetman served as coordinator of the photography program for the Penland School of Crafts; she returned to teaching in 1973-74 as a Visiting Professor at Rochester Institute of Technology and subsequently, in 1975, as Professor at University of Florida, until her retirement. Streetman often travels as a lecturer and has received fellowships from the National Endowment of the Arts and Fine Arts Council of Florida. Since the 1960s, she has exhibited her work in over a hundred solo and group exhibitions within the continental United States and abroad.

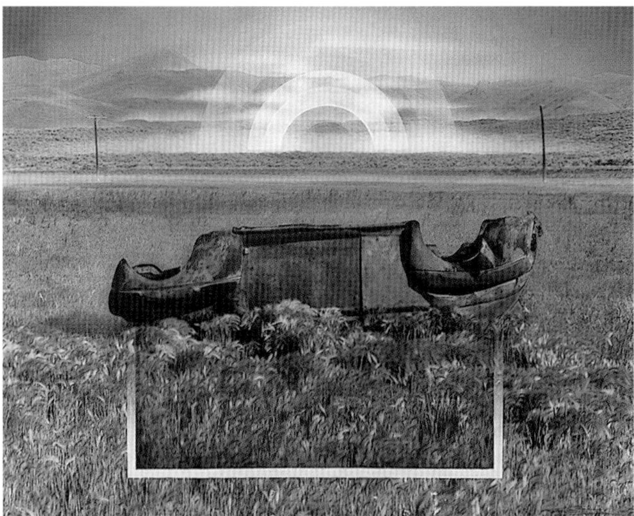

Evon Streetman, *Homage to James Agee*, 1979, Type C print, Kodak dyes and acrylic, 16x20 inches.

- Portrait of Lucy Rivers Murray, 1962, silver gelatin print, 10½x13 inches.
- Portrait of Isabelle Strauss Blakely, 1964, silver gelatin print, 9¾x11½ inches.
- Portrait of Bill Blakely, 1970, silver gelatin print, 9x9 inches.
- *Tribute to Wyeth*, 1975, silver gelatin print and graphite, 24x28 inches.
- *Idaho Landscape (Craters of the Moon)*, 1976, cibachrome and acrylic, 30x40 inches.
- *All American blueprint*, 1978, blueprint, hand coloring, 20x34 inches.
- *American Gothic blueprint*, 1978, blueprint, hand coloring, 22x30 inches.
- *Homage to James Agee*, 1979, Type C print, Kodak dyes and acrylic, 16x20 inches.
- *Penland Reflections*, 1983, mixed medium, 30x40 inches.
- *Reflections & Wisteria*, 1983, cibachrome and acrylic, 24x31 inches.
- *Rock and Reflections*, 1984, cibachrome, 40x30 inches.
- *Dream River #2*, 1991, mixed medium, 32x34 inches.
- *Falling Landscape*, 1991, cibachrome, 40x50 inches.
- *Landscape for Edith, II*, 1994, cibachrome, 40x50 inches.
- *Falling Landscape, II*, 1994, cibachrome, 40x50 inches.
- *Falling Landscape, IV*, 1994 , cibachrome, 40x50 inches.
- *Falling Landscape, III*, 1994, cibachrome, 40x50 inches.
- *Landscape for Harold*, 1994, cibachrome, 40x50 inches.
- *Landscape for Harold II*, 1994, cibachrome, 40x50 inches.

## TYLER TURKLE

Tyler Turkle was born May 29, 1947. He received his BA in history from Mount Union College in Ohio. From 1975 to 1987, he taught art, photography and filmmaking at Florida State University as a visiting lecturer, assistant professor and artist-in-residence. His films have appeared in national and international film festivals while his paintings and sculptures have been widely exhibited in museums and galleries throughout the United States and Europe. Turkle was selected for the 41st and 44th Biennial Exhibitions of Contemporary American Painting at the Corcoran Gallery of Art, Washington, DC, as well as exhibitions at the San Francisco Museum of Art, San Francisco, California; Stedelijk Museum, Amsterdam, the Netherlands; the Ringling Museum of Art, Sarasota, Florida; the Fort Worth Museum of Art, Fort Worth, Texas; the Rooseum, Malmo, Sweden; and the New Orleans Museum of Art, New Orleans, Louisiana. Turkle is actively involved in projects both nationally and locally. He is recognized as a volunteer filmmaker

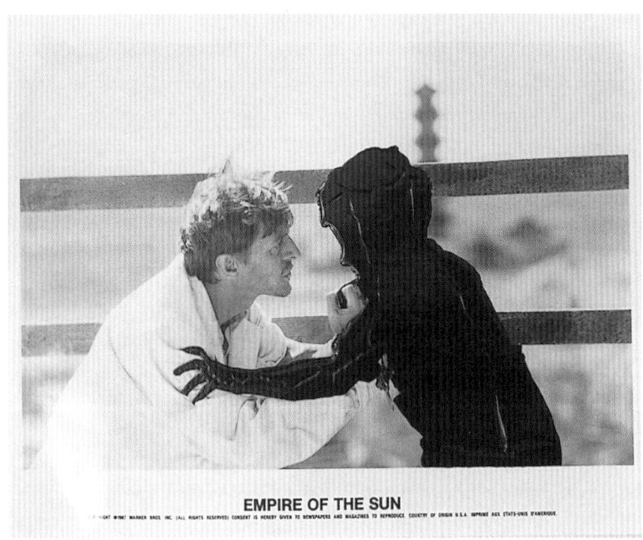


Tyler Turkle, *Untitled* from the Plastic Publicity series, 1984-1995, poured acrylic on B&W photo, 8x10 inches. Courtesy of Lance Kinz and Susan Reynolds, New York, New York.

for Stephen Spielberg's organization, Survivors of the SHOAH/ Visual History Foundation, and he has served as a trustee of the Edward F. Marsicano Literary Trust. Currently, Turkle is Executive Director of the Leon County Schools' Foundation and Artistic Director of the Tallahassee/Leon County Cultural Resources Commission.

- *Walk That Dog*,1974, B&W, 16mm Film (on VHS). Courtesy of Canyon Cinema, San Francisco, California.
- *Observeillance,* 1976, color, 16 mm film (on VHS). Courtesy of Canyon Cinema, San Francisco, California.
- *Mona Breakfast*, 1976, poured acrylic on velvet, 33x46 inches. Courtesy of Tricia Collins Contemporary Art, New York, New York.
- *Plastic Publicity*, 1984-95, poured acrylic on B&W photo, 8x10 inches each (seven pieces in total). Courtesy of Marsha Orr Contemporary Art, Tallahassee, Florida.
- *Artistic Anatomy*, 1985-89, 8½x12 inches each (seven pieces in total). Courtesy of Signature Gallery, Tallahassee, Florida.
- *Endless Marilyns*, 1986-87, poured acrylic mounted on plexiglas, 23x75 inches. Courtesy of Linda and Moses Rodin.
- *Sunset with Plastic #1*, 1990, poured acrylic on color photo, 40x60 inches. Courtesy of Tricia Collins Contemporary Art, New York, New York.
- *Curtains #8*, 1991, poured acrylic, 72x24 inches. Courtesy of Tricia Collins Contemporary Art, New York, New York.
- *Gators, Wrestlers, Football Players*, work in progress-1996 to present, Sony Beta SP (on VHS). Courtesy of Canyon Cinema, San Francisco, California.
- *Improved Last Criterion #2*, 2000, poured acrylic, 93x58 inches. Courtesy of Tricia Collins Contemporary Art, New York, New York.

## JERRY UELSMANN

Jerry Uelsmann was born in Detroit, Michigan, in 1934. He graduated from Rochester Institute of Technology with a BFA and Indiana University with an MS and an MFA. In 1960, he joined the faculty at the University of Florida, Gainesville. Uelsmann is recognized as a founding member of the Society for Photographic Education and a former trustee for the Friends of Photography. In 1967, he was awarded a Guggenheim Fellowship and a National Endowment of the Arts Fellowship in 1972. The Photographic Society of Japan presented him with

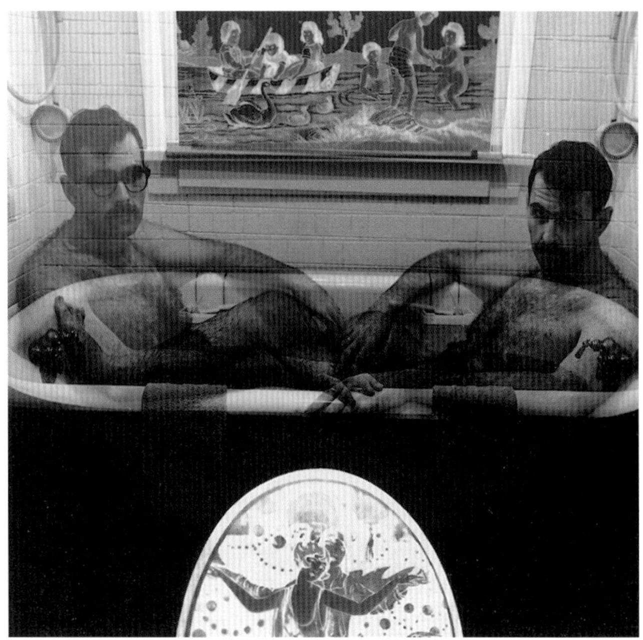

Jerry Uelsmann, *Self Portrait as Robinson and Rejlander*, 1964, photography, 16x20 inches.

an award for Outstanding Achievement and the University of Florida has recognized him as Teacher/Scholar of the Year (1975). Uelsmann's photographs have been exhibited worldwide, recently in such international cities as Paris and New York, and in exhibitions in Japan and Australia. Along with his exhibitions, Uelsmann has worked on numerous publications: *Museum Studies; Jerry Uelsmann: Photo Synthesis; Approaching the Shadow;* and others. In 1997, he retired from the University of Florida's Art Department, and continues to reside in Gainesville.

- *Symbolic Mutation*, 1961, silver gelatin print, 7x8 inches.
- *Room Number 1*, 1963, silver gelatin print, 16x20 inches.
- *Equivalent*, 1964, silver gelatin print, 16x20 inches.
- *Self Portrait as Robinson and Rejlander*, 1964, silver gelatin print, 16x20 inches.
- *Simultaneous Intimations*, 1965, silver gelatin print, 16x20 inches.
- *Magritte's Touchstone*, 1965, silver gelatin print, 16x20 inches.
- *Small Woods Where I Met Myself* (final version, 1967), silver gelatin print, 16x20 inches.
- *Apocalypse II*, 1967, silver gelatin print, 16x20 inches.
- *Turtle Blessing*, 1968, silver gelatin print, 16x20 inches.
- *Untitled (toned experiment—blue magnolia)*, 1968, silver gelatin print, 16x20 inches.
- *Untitled (floating tree)*, 1968, silver gelatin print, 16x20 inches.
- *Shaman's Study*, 1991, silver gelatin print, 16x20 inches.
- *Lost Questions*, 1991, silver gelatin print, 16x20 inches.
- *Untitled (Yosemite meditation)*, 1996, silver gelatin print, 16x20 inches.
- *Approaching the Shadow*, 1996, silver gelatin print,16x20 inches.
- *Untitled (boat and waterfall)*, 1997, silver gelatin print, 16x20 inches.
- *Memories of Max Ernst*, 1997, silver gelatin print, 16x20 inches.
- *Homage to Man Ray*, 1997, silver gelatin print, 16x20 inches.
- *Ancestral Journey*, 1998, silver gelatin print, 16x20 inches.
- *Mediation on the "I" and Eye of Joseph Cornell*, 1998, silver gelatin print, 16x20 inches.
- *Untitled (boat in clouds)*, 1998, silver gelatin print, 16x20 inches.
- *Riddle of Failure*, 1999, silver gelatin print, 16x20 inches.
- *Untitled (star fish, ladder)*, 1999, silver gelatin print, 16x20 inches.
- *Silent Shore*, silver gelatin print, 1999, 16x20 inches.
- *Sommer's Mandala*, 1999, silver gelatin print, 16x20 inches.
- *Undiscovered Self*, 1999, IRIS print, 29x34 inches.
- *Untitled (Tintern Abbey)*, 1999, IRIS print, 20x27 inches.
- *Homage to Duchamp*, 2000, silver gelatin print, 16x20 inches.

## TODD WALKER

Born in Salt Lake City on September 25, 1917, Todd Walker attended classes at Glendale Junior College and the Art Center School, Los Angeles. Subsequently, he began working as a photographer on educational films for Tradefilms, Inc. In 1946, he became a self-employed photographer for Burden/Walker Studio in Beverly Hills, California. While self-employed, Walker began teaching photography at Art Center College of Design, UCLA, and California State College. In 1970, he moved from California to Florida to become an Associate Professor at the University of Florida, Gainesville. Over the span of his career, Walker received two National Endowment of the Arts Photography Fellowships, a Florida Council for the Arts Photography Fellowship, and the Tucson Community Foundation, Buffalo Arts Award. His exhibition career began in the 1950s in the States, but works were in exhibitions abroad in

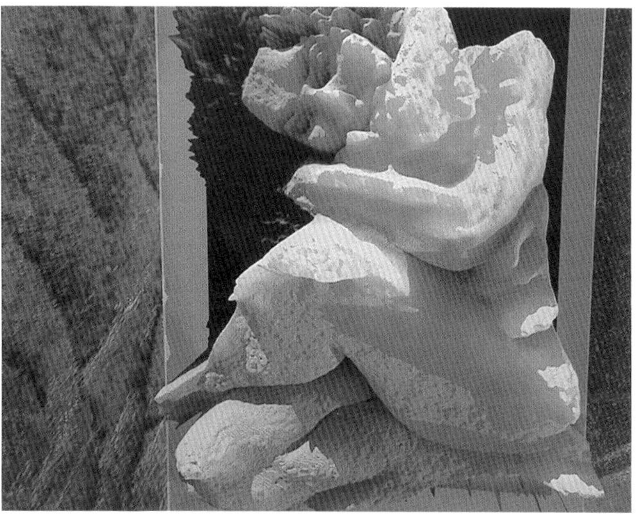

Todd Walker, *Nandax*, 1990s, Epson archival print, 12¼x15⅝ inches.

France and Italy, and were also in Mexico. In 1977, he accepted a teaching position at the University of Arizona, Tucson, and in 1985, retired as Professor Emeritus from the same university. Walker continued to live in Tucson until his death in 1998.

- *Chevy*, nd, silkscreen, ns.
- *Francine, dancing*, 1972, silkscreen, 14½x19 inches.
- *Chris, green*, 1972, silkscreen, 15½x19½ inches.
- *Sally, abstract orange*, 1972, silkscreen, 13x9¾ inches.
- *Tallahassee Trees*, 1973, silkscreen15¼x23 inches.
- *Palm Frond*, 1973, silkscreen, 13x17¾ inches.
- *To Linda Connor*, 1973, silkscreen, 14½x18½ inches.
- *Caroline and baby*, 1974, silkscreen, 9⅞x14¾ inches.
- *Becky N., woods*, 1974, silkscreen, 9¾x13¼ inches.
- *Gaver in cave*, 1977, silkscreen, 12 15/16x19¼ inches.
- *Feininger's stairs*, 1978, silkscreen, 9½x12 inches.
- *Marivir*, 1990s, Epson archival print, 12¼x15½ inches.
- *Swids2*, 1990s, Epson archival print, 12¼x16¼ inches.
- *Set1nan*, 1990s, Epson archival print, 12¼x16¼ inches.
- *Twinhed*, 1990s, Epson archival print, 12¼x16¼ inches.
- *Nandax*, 1990s, Epson archival print, 12¼x15⅝ inches.
- *alle*, 1990s, Epson archival print, 12¼x14⅝ inches.
- *L5ch*, 1990s, Epson archival print, 12¼x16¼ inches.
- *Tw71n*, 1990s, Epson archival print, 12¼x15½ inches.
- *Wraith*, 1990s, Epson archival print, 12¼x16¼ inches.
- *Deqpam*, 1990s, Epson archival print, 12¼x15½ inches.
- *A72-730*, nd, Epson archival print, 12¼x16¼ inches.
- *Bussmm*, nd, Epson archival print, 12¼x16¼ inches.
- *Annrep*, nd, Epson archival print, 12¼x16¼ inches.
- *Stmk*, nd, Epson archival print, 12¼x15⅝ inches.
- *NYCF*, nd, Epson archival print, 12¼x16¼ inches.
- *A Few Notes*, nd, book, 5½x6⅜ inches.
- *SEE*, nd, book, 5½x7 inches.
- *Binary Banana Book*, nd, book, 7x9 inches.
- *27 Photographs*, nd, book, 6x7¾ inches.
- *For Nothing Changes*, nd, book, 4¾x6 inches.

## WALLACE WILSON

Wallace Wilson was born in 1947. He began studying architectural design at Texas Tech University in Lubbock, Texas and obtained his BA in communication, film, television from the University of Texas at Austin. In 1970, he began working as an Instructor for the College of Architecture and as Head of the Photography Program at the University of Kentucky. While on staff there, he earned his MFA from the School of the Art Institute of Chicago. Wilson, who is now Chair of the Art Department at the University of South Florida, taught at other institutions including the University of Delaware, the University of Florida, and the University of Gothenburg in Sweden. He has been the recipient of a Florida Arts Council Individual Artist Fellowship and a Polaroid Corporation Invitational Fellowship, as well as receiving various research grants. Wilson's works have been exhibited internationally. He actively lectures and participates in workshops and conferences. He resides in the Tampa Bay area.

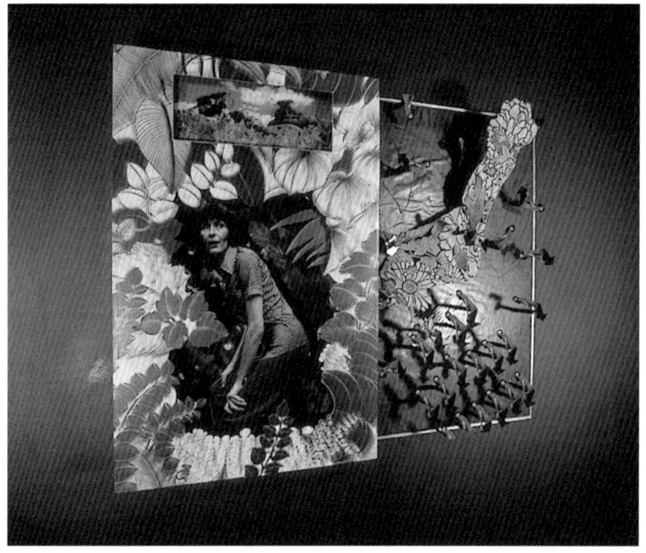

Wallace Wilson, *Fear of Nature*, 1983, installation view of photo relief assemblage, 30x40x6 inches.

- *Bird One*, 1979, color photograph, 20x24 inches.
- *Bird Two*, 1979, color photograph, 20x24 inches.
- *Nudist One*, 1979, color photograph, 20x24 inches.
- *Nudist Two*, 1979, color photograph, 20x24 inches.
- *Uneasy Emerging Enigma*, 1982, photo relief assemblage, 16x20x2 inches.
- *Fear of Nature*, 1983, photo relief assemblage, 30x40x6 inches.
- *New World Man*, 1983, photo relief assemblage, 40x30x6 inches.
- *Dog and Home*, 1984, silver gelatin print, 72x48 inches.
- *Jesus and Stieglitz*, 1985, Polaroid photograph, 20x24 inches.
- *He/She Switch*, 1985, Polaroid photograph,72x42 inches.

- *Guardians of Culture*, 1990, silver gelatin print, 70x48 inches. Collection: Southeast Museum of Photography, Daytona Beach Community College.
- *Urban Dinosaur*, 1988, silver gelatin print, 72x48 inches.
- *Baby Icon*, 1990, silver gelatin print, 70x47 inches.
- *Distorted Transmission*, 1996, backlighted digital color acetate photograph, 40x50 inches.

## DAVID YAGER

Born March 16, 1949, in Bronx, New York, David Yager earned his BA from the University of Connecticut / Storrs, and his MFA from Florida State University. After graduation, he worked at a series of different museums, including the Museum of Modern Art and the Museum of Fine Arts, Boston, as well as several universities, such as the Art Institute of Chicago, Columbia College (Chicago), and University of South Florida / Tampa. Yager was awarded a Florida Arts Council grant, and IBM and Apple Research Grants. In addition to numerous solo exhibitions, he participated in *Light*, Loch Haven Museum (now Orlando Museum of Art); *Magic Silver Show*, Washington, DC; and *Silver International*, University of South Florida. His works are in the permanent collections of the Museum of Modern Art, the Art Institute of Chicago, and the Metropolitan Museum of Art. In 1986, he accepted a position as Professor of Art at University of Maryland, Baltimore County, and founded the Imaging Research Center (IRC), an internationally recognized digital research facility. In 1994 he became Distinguished Professor of Art, a title he currently holds. Today, Yager shares the unique position of being both a UMBC Distinguished Professor and Executive Director of the Fine Arts Gallery, as well as President of Latitude360, a subsidiary of RWD Technologies and the director of RWD's Applied Technology Laboratory. This new laboratory will focus on the development of e-learning, e-commerce, and e-business. RWD and UMBC have initiated a strong relationship, which began two years ago with a major research grant to the IRC.

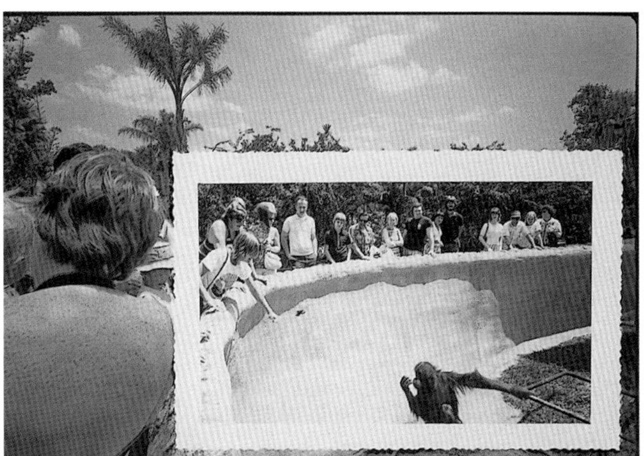

David Yager, from the series I Found You, 1980, silver gelatin print, 11x14 inches.

- from the series Hollywood #101, 1972-73, silver gelatin print, 11x14 inches.
- from the series Hollywood, 1972-73, silver gelatin print, 11x14 inches.
- from the series Parade, 1974-75, silver gelatin print, 11x14 inches.
- from the series Dogland #221, 1975, cyanotype and gum bichromate, 29x28 inches.
- from the series Consumption #7, 1977, Type C print, 30x30 inches.
- from the series I Found You #2, 1980, silver gelatin print, 11x14 inches.
- from the series I Found You, 1980, silver gelatin print, 11x14 inches.
- Untitled, 1986, Type C print, 96x38 inches.
- from the series Goals and Roles #115, 1987, lithograph, 96x38 inches.
- from the series Goals and Roles #116, 1987, lithograph, 96x38 inches.
- from the series Lost Souls #9, 1992, silver gelatin print, hand-colored, 20x40 inches.
- from the series Lost Souls #21, 1993, silver gelatin print, hand-colored, 20x40 inches.
- from the series Education, Medicine, Science 1999 #105, 1999, Type C print, 29x28 inches.
- from the series Education, Medicine, Science 1999 #107, 1999, Type C print, 29x28 inches.
- from the series Education, Medicine, Science 1999 #112, 1999, Type C print, 29x28 inches.
- from the series Education, Medicine, Science 1999 #132, 1999, Type C print, 29x28 inches.

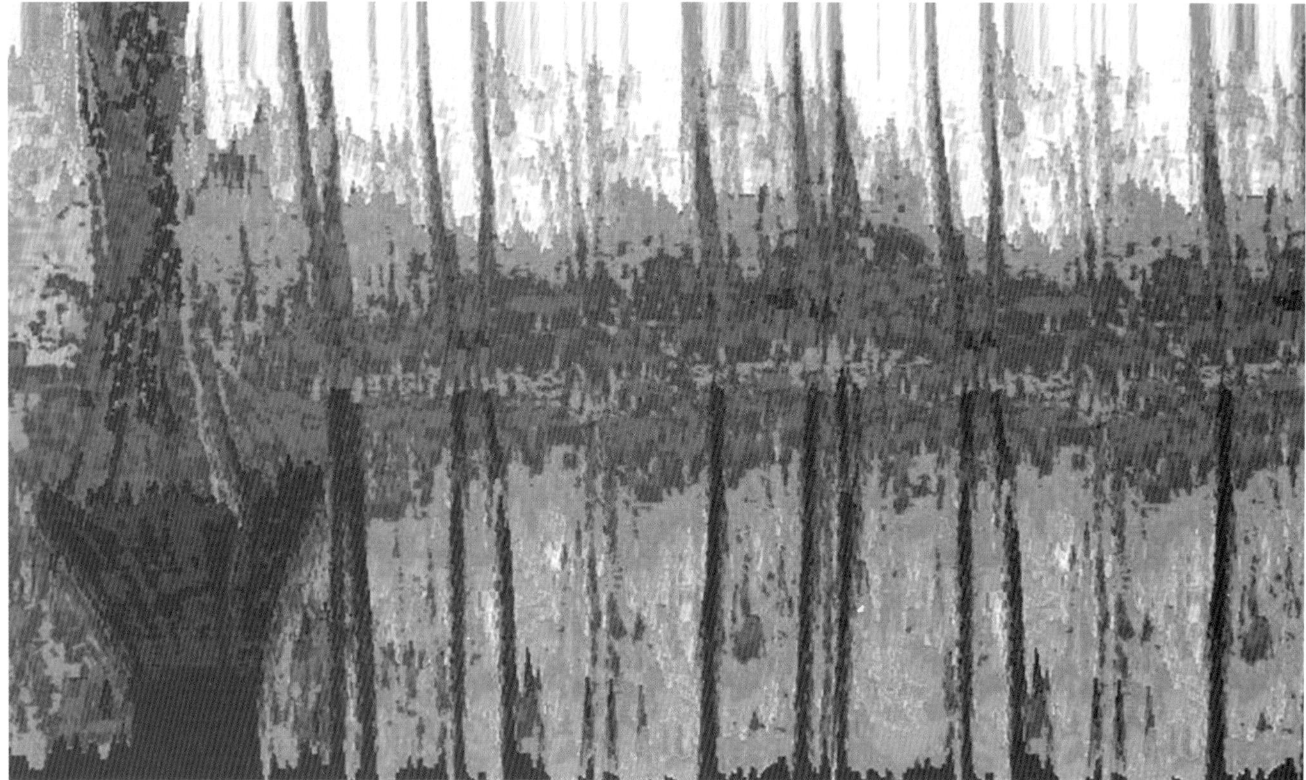

Todd Walker, *The Swamp*, digital file, c. 1990s. Courtesy of the Todd Walker Estate.

*I am a photographer, firmly grounded in the California tradition of straightforward camera work and the fine print. That is where I learned photography and how I worked for many years. The function of working with a camera is to produce not merely an image, as it is popularly called, but also a picture. A dictionary defines what I mean by those words:*

*Image: The optical counterpart of an object produced by the lens.*

*Picture: The representation of something in visible or symbolic form.*

*For me, the image formed by the camera often needs to be transformed into a picture. This transformation is an important part of my work. In addition to being involved with the image while using the camera, I find it necessary to concentrate that image, to make apparent the illusions I carry about my environment and to form a concrete picture that attempts to describe and delineate my illusion.*

*When, from among the many incomplete or inadequate pictures I have done, one seems to support the illusion I had while using the camera, or that it may now bring to my mind, this becomes the particular one from which I evolve my representation of that illusion.*

*Representation: To present again.*

*This representation of the picture has had certain restrictions during the course of my career, as well as during the short history of photography. I have attempted to leave those restrictions behind me.*

*My concerns still incorporate the unique ability of the camera and lens to reveal subtle differences in tone that result when light is absorbed and reflected by things of the world, and the marvelous extension of vision that this makes possible.*

*I came to photography with the desire to conquer the camera and make it my slave. Instead I now have a respect for this machine and other machines as true expanders of my awareness as well as my vision. The printing press, the process camera, and now the computer are teaching me that other pictures are possible than those of which I was aware.*

*Through all of this I am trying to make pictures, to re-present something in visual or symbolic form.*

Todd Walker
(1917-1998)